Rebecca Probert read law at St Anne's College, Oxford and took her LLM at University College, London. She worked as a researcher at the Law Commission, and has lectured in family law since 1997. She is currently Professor of Law at the University of Warwick and is a leading authority on the history of the marriage laws of England and Wales, a subject on which she has written extensively.

Also by Rebecca Probert

Marriage Law and Practice in the Long Eighteenth Century: A Reassessment (CUP, 2009).

'The word "groundbreaking" is, for once, an accurate description…. Professor Probert comprehensively trashes the work of many scholars (including some of great eminence) who have written about marriage and the family—indeed some of them might think they should hand back their honorary degrees and many more will breathe sighs of relief that research funding once granted cannot in practice be reclaimed.' (*International Journal of Law in Context*)

'Every so often comes along a book which challenges long-established orthodoxies; this is one such publication…. The arguments advanced are… both convincing and compelling.' (*Ecclesiastical Law Journal*)

the rights & wrongs of royal marriage

*how the law has led to
heartbreak, farce and confusion,
and why it must be changed*

TAKEAWAY

2011

First published in Great Britain in 2011
by Takeaway (Publishing)

1st edition, 1st rev.

Takeaway (Publishing), 33 New Street, Kenilworth CV8 2EY

E-mail: books@takeawaypublishing.co.uk

British Library Cataloguing in Publication Data.
A catalogue record for this book is available from the British Library

ISBN 978-0-9563847-3-7

Design by Shine Design

Contents

chapter 1

Introduction

A PRINCELY MARRIAGE is the brilliant edition of a universal fact, proclaimed the essayist Walter Bagehot upon the wedding of the future King Edward VII in 1863, 'and as such it rivets mankind.' The Archbishop of Canterbury, Robert Runcie, quoted those very same words upon the marriage of Prince Charles and Lady Diana Spencer more than a century later.[1] The public of course had little hope of witnessing the first of these two ceremonies—even some of the dignitaries who had travelled to Windsor Castle could not be accommodated within the confines of St George's Chapel to view the exchange of vows[2]—but the romances of Edward's great-great-grandson were subjected to far greater media scrutiny,[3] and in 1981 an estimated 750 million viewers in 74 countries around the world watched the wedding being broadcast live from St Paul's Cathedral.[4] As an eight-year-old child growing up in a village in the English Midlands, my personal interest was engaged by the cakes my mother had made for the occasion. A trio of school friends and I sat solemnly licking the red, white and blue icing and watching events unfold on the television. I played at weddings for weeks afterwards, with a Sindy doll dressed in white and a rather out-of-scale groom.

Three decades on, and with the wedding of Prince William and Kate Middleton in Westminster Abbey the attention of the world's media has once again been riveted upon a princely marriage.[5] With the engagement of Zara Phillips to the rugby player Mike Tindall also being announced in late 2010, and a new generation of royal offspring reaching marriageable age, more royal weddings can be expected in the coming years. Now, however, I find myself surrounded by law books rather than dolls, and my interest in royal weddings lies more in the rules that underpin them than in their grand spectacle. For in one crucial respect the marriages of members of the royal family are not simply 'a brilliant edition of a universal fact,' as Walter Bagehot and Robert Runcie proclaimed. For centuries there have been distinct rules governing royal marriages—whom they may marry, when they may marry, and how they may marry—which do not govern the marriages of the general public.

Thus for over three hundred years it has been the law that any member of the royal family who marries a Catholic will forfeit his or her right to the throne; a large number of royal descendants—exactly how large remains a matter of great uncertainty—require the consent of the sovereign in order to be capable of marrying; and, at least until the marriage of the Prince of Wales in 2005, it was understood that members of the royal family were only permitted to marry according to the rites of the Church of England (at least in England and Wales), for the simple reason that the legislation that introduced other modes of marrying was specifically stated not to apply to them.[6]

Such restrictions—for restrictions they undeniably are—have been widely criticized as being out of kilter with the modern law's emphasis on equality and freedom of choice, and there have been numerous attempts by individual MPs at reform. The events of 2005, however, raised more serious and immediate questions. When it was announced in January of that year that Prince Charles would marry Camilla Parker Bowles in a civil marriage ceremony rather than before an Anglican minister, various legal experts—myself included—publicly questioned whether the law actually made provision for such a possibility.

Regrettably, the cavalier way in which these objections were addressed by the government of the day has meant that questions continue to be raised about the validity of the civil wedding that eventually took place in Windsor Guildhall on April 9th, 2005. Even now, certain quarters of the media will every so often report on yet another legal document that casts doubt on the possibility of a royal civil marriage. And, predictably, the announcement of the engagement of Charles' eldest son William provided the opportunity to reopen the issue. 'It was not so simple for Charles,' mused one journalist, before going on to provide a blow-by-blow account of the problems that had dogged that earlier wedding.[7]

One cannot but have sympathy for the individuals in question, whose love and affection for each other is apparent, when their marriage continues to be so fruitlessly impugned in this way. Nothing in the pages that follow is intended to cast doubt on the status of Charles and Camilla's marriage: while there were serious and valid doubts at the time as to whether they were entitled to marry in a civil ceremony, the marriage went ahead with the authority of the Registrar-General, and there is now no means by which it can be challenged. English marriage law tends to be pragmatic, and it is perfectly possible for legal effects to flow from a ceremony that should not, according to the letter of that law, have gone ahead.[8] The Prince of Wales and the Duchess of Cornwall are married in the eyes of the law, and there need be no more side-swipes at the validity of their union.

But that is not to say that the events of 2005 are irrelevant. Far from it. The assurances of the then Lord Chancellor, Lord Falconer, that members of the royal family were entitled to marry in a civil ceremony—or indeed, by inference, in any of the statutory forms available to the general public—raised more questions than it answered. Where, then, does his reasoning leave the law on *future* royal marriages?

Let me give an example to illustrate the problems which the events of 2005 have raised. If, as Lord Falconer implied, the general law of marriage does now apply to members of the royal family just as it applies to members of the public, does this mean that they are similarly bound by its restrictions, as well as being able to take advantage of its options? In other words, what would happen if members of the royal family failed to comply with the law in circumstances where a court would declare void the marriage of less elevated persons? One would assume, of course, that members of the royal family would receive the very best legal advice on such vital matters, rendering such non-compliance extremely unlikely. Yet the initial announcement that the wedding of the Prince of Wales was to take place in Windsor Castle—which was not a venue that had been approved for civil marriages and which could not have obtained the appropriate approval in sufficient time—indicates that it cannot be taken for granted that sound and informed legal advice will be forthcoming.

A further and more pertinent question was raised by Lord Falconer's invocation of the Human Rights Act to justify his interpretation of the legislation on marriage. If, as he announced in a written statement to the House of Lords, the general law of marriage now has to be read in a way that is compatible with the Human Rights Act, does that same rule also apply to the far more discriminatory provisions relating to royal marriage to a Catholic, or to the statutory restrictions whereby a royal marriage is void if celebrated without the monarch's consent? After all, the effect of these rules is potentially far more dramatic: had it been decided that Charles and Camilla were not entitled to marry in a civil ceremony in England and Wales, there would have been nothing to stop them from marrying in Scotland, or indeed overseas, or in front of a willing Anglican minister if one could be procured; by contrast, a marriage celebrated without the consent of the Queen would have been void wherever or however it was celebrated.

Given the considerable doubt about the scope and application of the existing law on royal marriage, and with a number of young royals expected to marry in the coming years, it is important that these issues should receive full and serious consideration. While broad discussion has not been lacking, royal correspondents and biographers tend in the main not to have any legal training, and mistakes and misunderstandings as to the scope of the different rules are all too common.[9]

Not that this is anything new. As one legal commentator noted as long ago as 1811, 'hasty opinions have been precipitately formed—fallacious impressions imbibed—and conclusions also adopted, without due consideration of fundamental principles.'[10] Unfortunately, subsequent readers clearly disagreed with his arguments as to those fundamental principles, for the copy in the British Library bears many scribbled comments, large crosses, angry blots and tetchy notes of 'Nonsense!' I trust that readers will not be provoked to similar reactions by the pages that follow: my aim is to provide a clear and authoritative explanation of how the law has developed, to demonstrate the uncertainties that exist and the problems that have resulted, and to advance proposals for reform.

The first part of this book sets out how the peculiar set of rules applicable to royal marriages has developed. Chapter two examines the circumstances that led to adverse consequences being attached to any marriage to a Catholic, and chapter three the unsuitable matches that inspired greater controls over the marriages of members of the royal family. Chapter four traces the parallel evolution of the general law of marriage to show why members of the royal family were exempted from the terms of Lord Hardwicke's Act of 1753, the first statute to regulate entry into marriage, and looks at how that exemption—intended at the time as a royal privilege—ultimately became a problematic restriction.

One key theme of chapters three and four is the impact of these restrictions in the twentieth century, in particular on those members of the royal family who had failed to find happiness in their first marriages and who wished to remarry, or who had fallen in love with a divorcee. Such people faced a problem: throughout the twentieth century the Church of England generally refused to conduct the marriage of any divorced persons, even those who had not been responsible for the breakdown of the marriage, at least while their ex-spouse was still alive (indeed, when my own parents married in 1971 they were obliged to do so in a register office, despite the fact that my father's first marriage had come to an end on account of his first wife's adultery). So, given that members of the royal family could not marry in a civil ceremony in England and Wales, what were divorcees to do? Renunciation of royal status was one option, as the case of Princess Margaret will illustrate, but not a particularly enticing one. Marriage outside the jurisdiction was another, and one taken by an increasing number of royals from the 1960s onwards.

A third option, adopted by Lord Falconer in 2005, was simply to try to reinterpret the relevant legislation, and that approach is subjected to detailed scrutiny in chapter five. The significance of the interpretation advanced by Lord Falconer is not only its application to all future royal marriages but also the fact that it calls into question the remaining rules. Chapter six is therefore devoted to considering the uncertainties and complexities of the current law, which have been exacerbated rather than ameliorated by the events of 2005. It also considers how reforms could best be enacted in order to bring the law relating to royal marriage into the twenty-first century.

Such criticisms of the laws on royal marriage should not be mistaken for criticism of the royal family. I have every sympathy for the invidious position in which members of the royal family have found themselves, and hope that this exposition of the laws will assist in bringing about reform. In the pages that follow I aim to avoid both the delight in muck-raking that characterizes many lurid accounts of the sex-lives of royals past or present, and the deference that has in the past led to possible reforms being dropped as too embarrassing. To quote that commentator of 1811 once more: 'these pages have been written without the solicitation, the knowledge, the expectation or the privity of any individual—with a view solely of promoting the ends of justice.'[11]

It may be objected that the rules relating to marriages of members of the royal family *should* be different, whether because they are expected to set an example to the rest of society, or because their marriages are of public importance and there is a price to be paid for privileges. But this objection is easily countered. For one thing, the current rules apply to many obscure members of the royal family who bear no title and who will never ascend to the throne. There can be no justifiable reason for subjecting the marriages of these individuals to special treatment. More importantly, it can be argued that the restrictions applying to members of the royal family were not intended to form a distinct set of rules—or at least not as distinct as they are today. At the time that the relevant laws were passed, similar restrictions applied to the populace as a whole. The general law of marriage has since moved on—but the law applicable to members of the royal family has not.

It should also be noted that members of the royal family have not, contrary to what is popularly thought, enjoyed any special privileges with regard to the *ending* of their marriages. Nor has there ever been any specific law preventing a member of the royal family from divorcing, marrying a divorced person, or remarrying after a divorce. The difficulties faced by Henry VIII in wishing to free himself of an unwanted spouse were not unique to members of the royal family. Divorce—in the modern sense of an order ending a valid marriage—was not legally available to anyone in sixteenth-century England, and an annulment—a declaration that the marriage had never existed—could only be granted in a limited range of circumstances.[12] Admittedly King Henry did face an extra obstacle—his wife Catherine was aunt to the Holy Roman Emperor—but this was a problem of politics, not law. Nor indeed did Henry obtain a divorce even *after* breaking with Rome: his marriages to Catherine of Aragon, Anne Boleyn and Anne of Cleves were all ended by annulments. It was not until the late seventeenth century that the first true divorce—ending a valid marriage rather than declaring the marriage not to have existed in the first place—was granted by Parliament.[13] King George IV tried to avail himself of this procedure in order to ensure that his wife Caroline did not become Queen, but he failed. While it might only have been in 1967, 110 years after divorce had become judicially available, that a member of the royal family (the Earl of Harewood) actually took advantage of the statute, the possibility had never formally been denied to them.

It should also be noted that many aspects of royal marriage have *not* been regulated—or, rather, have been regulated other than by formal statutes. There has, for example, never been a legal requirement that royalty should only marry royalty. Nonetheless, before the twentieth century, intermarriage with the various ruling dynasties of continental Europe was the norm. There were, of course, exceptions: the younger brother of Charles II married plain old Anne Hyde (though she died before he ascended the throne as James II). But the House of Hanover was jealous of its status, and from the start of the eighteenth century a consort of royal blood was regarded as the only acceptable match.[14] Marriage was a form of diplomacy, a means of cementing alliances between nations, and the personal happiness of the parties was incidental.

Wider expectations of married life have, of course, changed enormously since the eighteenth century. The Royal Marriages Act of 1772 may have been passed with the aim of ensuring that princes and princesses married only royals of equal rank, but aristocratic parents too would have been equally keen to ensure that their offspring married only within their class, and equally unconcerned with compatibility of temperament. And all the way down the social scale, class was a crucial factor in determining the range of potential mates.

Today—and many books and academic treatises have been devoted to determining when precisely this change occurred—love has become the only respectable motivation for marriage, and we regard as suspect those whose unions are motivated by lucre or the lure of celebrity. An eighteenth-century Anna Nicole Smith would have been regarded as having made a 'good match'; a twenty-first century Elizabeth Bennett would be condemned as mercenary if she tweeted that she found Mr Darcy much more likeable after seeing the size of his house. If we do expect members of the royal family to set us an example of proper behaviour, then the nature of that example has to be determined by the values of society today, rather than that of two hundred years ago.

But it is not my intention to engage in debate as to *whom* members of the royal family ought to be able to marry, but *how*. Of course I have my own views on the former, but am ever wary of those who spin opinion into assertion. On how it is possible to marry, however, I can lay claim to considerable expertise. The pages that follow are grounded in over a decade's-worth of research on eighteenth-century marriage law and practice, examining legal disputes, contemporary treatises, archival sources and literary texts. Such work is not merely valuable background for understanding the context in which the current laws on royal marriages evolved. If members of the royal family are still exempt from the general law of marriage as laid down by statute, then it becomes essential to know what the law was before such statutory intervention, since this is the law that will apply to members of the royal family. My work in this area is widely regarded as having transformed previous understandings of the law,[15] and casts doubt on some of the suggestions advanced during the controversy over Charles and Camilla's civil marriage in 2005.

When I first embarked on a study of eighteenth-century marriage law, it was as a matter of academic curiosity; I had no expectation that it would prove to be of such direct relevance. The events of 2005 took me out of the archives and onto the airwaves; the events of 2011 provide an opportunity to open up for debate once more the question of whether universal rules should apply to princely marriages.

chapter 2

The Act of Settlement and the Consequences of Marrying a Catholic

IT WAS a birth, rather than a marriage, that prompted the last major disruption to the throne. After no fewer than five stillbirths and the deaths of five further children in early infancy, the second wife of King James II had given birth to a baby boy on June 10th, 1688. But the King's existing daughter Mary and her husband William of Orange refused to accept the birth as legitimate. Rumours abounded of boy babies being smuggled into the royal bedchamber in a warming pan. Given that the birth of James Francis Edward had (as was customary) been witnessed by dozens, including the entire Privy Council, any such substitution would have required considerable sleight of hand.[1] But why should the birth of this particular royal baby have been a cause for doubt in the first place? The problem was that his father, King James II, was a convert to Catholicism. England had not had an openly Catholic monarch for over a hundred years, and the fact that she was remembered by the nickname 'Bloody Mary' tells its own tale.

It can be difficult for modern readers unfamiliar with the religious politics of the day to appreciate the depth of anti-Catholic feeling in seventeenth-century England and the extent to which this was institutionalized in the law. Catholics were subject to penal laws[2] and could not practise their religion freely. Even harbouring a Catholic priest was a serious offence, and by the late seventeenth century Catholicism was very much a minority religion, surviving only where manors continued to be held by old Catholic families.[3] Only fifteen years before the birth of the baby James Francis Edward, Parliament had passed the Test Act, requiring anybody occupying public office to swear oaths of loyalty, take communion in the Church of England, and 'sign a declaration against the key Catholic belief of transubstan- tiation.' The future James II, at the time the brother of the then monarch King Charles II, had resigned his post as Lord Admiral rather than swear any such oaths. But the issue raised a difficult question. As the historian David Starkey has put it: 'if, as a Roman Catholic, James could not be Lord Admiral, how could he be entrusted with the infinitely greater respon- sibility of kingship?'[4]

Part of the reason for King James II's unpopularity was that since becoming monarch in 1685 he had set about removing some of the legal disadvantages affecting his co-religionists. Over in France, the Catholic King Louis XIV had revoked the previous policy of tolerating Protestants, leading to concerns that James might follow suit in England.[5] There had already been one serious attempt at an uprising against James, the Monmouth Rebellion, but it had been bloodily suppressed. So the birth of a son and heir for King James II was not the reason for the crisis, but it certainly provided an urgent pretext to act. It led to William of Orange being invited to come to England by those opposed to James, ostensibly—and controversially—to ensure Parliament's freedom from royal interference. William accordingly came, and with a large army in tow. James fled, and was subsequently deemed to have abdicated.

It was against this background that the subsequent English Bill of Rights was drafted. Proclaiming that 'it hath beene found by experience that it is inconsistent with the safety and welfaire of this protestant kingdome to be governed by a popish prince or by any King or Queene marrying a papist', it went on to provide that any Catholic, or anyone who had married a Catholic, would be precluded from succeeding to the throne.[6]

Although William and his wife Mary ascended the throne as joint rulers, the succession was complicated by the fact that Mary, as the legitimate daughter of King James II by his first wife, had a better claim to the throne than her husband William. It was agreed that Mary's descendants would succeed to the throne, followed by her younger sister Anne and her descendants, and only then any that William might sire by any other woman after Mary's death. In the event, though, this all proved academic: Mary died childless, and William did not remarry. Tragically, Anne's son died at the age of eleven, and despite her many pregnancies no other child had survived infancy.

With the death of Anne's son in 1700 it was clear that further steps needed to be taken to safeguard the succession and ensure the continuation of Protestant rule. Anne's younger half-brother James was as resolutely Catholic as his father, James II. James II's younger sister Minette, meanwhile, had married Philippe, Duke of Orleans, and her descendants had married into the Catholic monarchies of Europe. And so, in order to find a Protestant heir to the throne, it was necessary to go all the way back to 1603 and the first of the Stuart monarchs of Great Britain, King James I. James I's daughter Elizabeth had married the King of Bohemia. Their daughter, Princess Sophia, was still alive in 1700, having reached the age of 70. And, happily, Sophia had a son, George, who in turn had a son: the Protestant succession was secure.

But in fixing on Sophia and her descendants it was necessary to disregard no fewer than fifty other men and women with better claims to the throne (a figure which seemed so unlikely when first I read it that I spent several hours poring over books of genealogy to identify those in question, but which in fact turned out to be an *under*estimate). Given the compelling claim to the throne of King James II's son, the Catholic James Francis Edward, it was necessary to legislate. The Act of Settlement of 1701 warned the populace that it was 'absolutely necessary for the safety, peace and quiet of this realm to obviate all doubts and contentions in the same by reason of any pretended titles to the crown', and it provided that the succession would fall to Sophia and her heirs. It also reiterated the ban on any monarch 'hold[ing] communion with the see or church of Rome' and excluded from the succession any who 'profess the popish religion or shall marry a papist.'

Sophia herself never succeeded to the throne of England. She died in June, 1714, at the ripe old age of 83, just weeks before Queen Anne succumbed to a fatal stroke. Upon Anne's death, Sophia's son succeeded to the throne as King George I, after whose death male heir succeeded male heir down to the death of King George IV in 1830.

The impact of the Act of Settlement on the succession

Since the dramatic events of the late seventeenth and early eighteenth centuries, very few people have in fact been barred from the succession under the terms of the Act of Settlement. Those who have chosen to marry a Catholic have tended to have little chance of inheriting the throne (short of a tragedy on the scale found only in soap operas, or, as the 1991 comedy *King Ralph* suggested, electrocution in a freak accident while posing en masse for a royal family photograph). Prince Michael of Kent, for example, was eighth in line to the throne when he married the Catholic Baroness Marie-Christine von Reibnitz in 1978, while the Earl of St Andrews was even further removed from the succession when he married Sylvana Tomaselli in 1988. Lord Nicholas Windsor, who wed Paola Doimi de Frankopan in 2006,[7] had already converted to Catholicism on his own account,[8] and would in any case be no closer than 29th in line to the throne.

Others have chosen to give up their Catholic faith when marrying into the royal family: Autumn Kelly, who married Peter Phillips in 2008, had been baptized as a Catholic but was received into the Church of England before the marriage took place. This of course raises questions as to how the law defines who exactly counts as a 'Catholic' for these purposes.[9] The Act of Settlement, for example, requires the monarch to be 'in communion' with the Church of England, but does not—and arguably cannot—impose any stipulations as to privately held beliefs. In 1839 there was controversy over the fact that Lord Melbourne omitted to describe Prince Albert as being from 'a Protestant country' when announcing the intended marriage with Queen Victoria. The justification was that at least some members of the Coburg royal family were Catholic, but the omission was sufficient to lead to rumours about Albert's religious loyalties.[10]

The fact that those marrying Catholics have stood little chance of inheriting the throne has given successive governments an excuse not to reform the law, an exercise which would involve a great deal of national soul-searching and constitutional unpicking, not to mention inflaming parts of the United Kingdom where religious loyalty is still a divisive issue. Others have felt, however, that the use of offensively sectarian language in a key constitutional document demands reform regardless of the impact. In recent years a number of proposals for change have been put forward, and their fate will be considered further in chapter six.

Having said that those members of the royal family who have married Catholics have in any case been unlikely to inherit the throne, there was, however, one royal marriage to a Catholic that would have affected the succession had it not been for the effect of the second piece of legislation that we are interested in, and to which we shall now turn.

chapter 3

The Royal Marriages Act and the Need for the Monarch's Consent

I T IS inherently unsatisfactory,' wrote an exasperated civil servant in 1956, 'that personal and constitutional questions of such high importance should still depend on the operation of an 18th Century Statute which was admittedly passed hurriedly and in the face of considerable opposition, to deal with an ad hoc situation created largely by the unsatisfactory conduct of King George III's brothers.'[1] His indictment is an all-too-accurate account of the genesis of the Royal Marriages Act of 1772, and gives some indication of the criticisms that have been levelled at it since its passage. Uncertain in its scope, yet drastic in its effect, for some members of the royal family the Royal Marriages Act has been an irksome formality, while for others it has posed an obstacle to their happiness.

So what was the catalyst for such a piece of legislation? George III (king from 1760 to 1820) had strong views on how members of the royal family should conduct themselves. Deciding against marriage to Lady Sarah Lennox, he wrote that:

> 'The interest of my country shall ever be my first case... I am born for the happiness or misery of a great nation, and consequently must often act contrary to my passion.'[2]

His brothers, however, turned out to be rather more in thrall to their passions. William, Duke of Gloucester, married Maria Walpole, Dowager-Countess Lady Waldegrave, in a private ceremony at her house in 1766. The marriage was kept a secret: although Maria was the granddaughter of the eminent statesman Sir Robert Walpole, she was nevertheless the product of an extra-marital liaison between his son

Edward and a milliner's assistant, Dorothy Clement,[3] and was therefore not, in the eyes of the royal family, a suitable consort for a Prince. When George III eventually discovered the marriage, William was given the choice of appearing at court without his wife—or not at all. He chose the latter.[4]

But it was the marriage of the King's younger brother Henry, Duke of Cumberland, which provoked the King to act. Henry's marriage to the Hon. Anne Horton, which took place in 1771, was unlikely to be welcomed by the rest of the royal family.[5] Described as 'somewhat shady' by one biographer[6] and 'coarse and vulgar' by others, Anne's antecedents were far from respectable. Although her father was a member of the peerage, he was himself illegitimate, and was described by a contemporary observer as 'this hoary lecher.'[7] But Anne's attractions for Cumberland can easily be guessed at: she was, apparently, 'disarmingly alluring.'[8]

When the King learned of his brother's marriage he was understandably irate. 'In any country a Prince marrying a subject is looked upon as dishonourable,' he wrote to his brother William. 'But here where the crown is but too little respected it must be big with the greatest mischiefs.'[9] The King took the step of initiating legislation to ensure that he and any subsequent monarch would be able to prevent such scandalous matches from occurring, and the resulting Bill was presented to the House of Commons on March 4th, 1772.

The passage of the Royal Marriages Act

The preamble to the subsequent Act for the Better Regulating the Future Marriages of the Royal Family (to give it its full name) acknowledged that it had been inspired by the King's 'paternal affection' to his family and his 'royal concern for the future welfare' of the populace as a whole. It went on to proclaim that 'marriages in the royal family are of the highest importance to the state' and that Parliament had therefore been convinced of the 'wisdom and expediency' of establishing more effective regulation 'to guard the descendants of his late Majesty King George the Second... from marrying without the approbation of your Majesty, your heirs or successors, first had and obtained.'

As the allusion to 'more effective regulation' might suggest, the monarch did already enjoy *some* control over the marriages of members of the royal family. In 1717, a panel of judges had advised George III's great-grandfather, George I, that to him belonged 'the education and care of the persons of his Majesty's grandchildren... and the care and approbation of their marriages when grown up.'[10] Only a few days before the Royal Marriages Bill was introduced into Parliament, the House of Lords had delivered its opinion that under the common law the King had 'the Care and Approbation' of the marriages of his children and grand-children, and of the presumptive heir to the Crown,[11] save for 'the issue of princesses married into foreign families.' It had, however, admitted that 'to what other Branches of the Royal Family such Care and Approbation extend, we do not find precisely determined.' The important implication was that the King enjoyed no right of control over the marriages of his siblings. More importantly, even though the common law accorded him the 'care' of the marriages of his children and grandchildren, a marriage celebrated without his consent and knowledge would not thereby be void.[12] In short, the common law allowed the monarch to make marriages, but not to unmake them once they had been entered into.

Not everyone was convinced that there was a need for new legislation to give George III additional powers of control over royal marriages. The waspish diarist Horace Walpole commented that 'Never was an act passed *against* which so much, and *for* which so little, was said.' There was widespread opposition to the Act within Parliament, despite the barely-veiled threat from the King that he would 'expect a hearty support from everyone in my service and shall remember defaulters.'[13] Indeed, the King's request for legislation of this kind was itself the basis for much of the opposition, raising as it did the question of the relationship between Crown and Parliament and the powers each could exercise.

After much debate, the Bill passed the House of Commons by 168 votes to 115, although Sir Joseph Mawbey proposed an amendment that it should be described as 'an Act for enlarging and extending the prerogatives of the Crown, and for the encouragement of adultery and fornication.'[14] And opposition in the House of Lords was equally intense. Two decades earlier, it had largely been members of the House of Commons that had voiced objections against the Clandestine Marriages Act of 1753, while those in the House of Lords had supported the principle that parents should be able to exercise greater control over the marriages of their children. But members of the House of Lords were of course more liable to meet—and thus potentially to marry—members of the royal family, and thus had an interest in ensuring that there were no extra controls on such marriages.

But self-interest was not the only basis for the protests. Thirteen peers (and the Bishop of Bangor) took the step of recording their protest against the Act

'that it may stand recorded to that posterity which may suffer from the mischievous consequences of this Act, that we have no part in the confusions and calamities brought upon them, by rendering uncertain the succession to the Crown.'

They pointed out that the Act was badly drafted, did not apply to a reigning monarch ('the marriage, of all others, the most important to the public'), and, in encompassing all of the descendants of George II, would over time apply to 'a great number of people.'

All of these are pertinent criticisms of the Act, to which I shall return when considering the case for reform. But for now I shall turn to the actual provisions of the statute and consider its effects down to the present day.

The terms of the Royal Marriages Act

The Royal Marriages Act 1772 was blunt in its terms and drastic in its effect. It stated clearly that descendants of King George II would not be *capable* of marrying 'without the previous consent of his Majesty... signified under the great seal, and declared in council.' Having set out provisions for the recording of such consent, it went on to stipulate that 'every marriage, or matrimonial contract, of any [descendant of George II] without such consent first had and obtained, shall be null and void to all intents and purposes whatsoever.'[15] The monarch acquired absolute control over the marriages of all who fell within the specified category, at least until the individual in question reached the age of 25. Those over the age of 25 could contract a valid marriage against the sovereign's wishes twelve months after giving notice to the Privy Council of their desire to marry 'unless both Houses of Parliament... expressly declare their disapprobation of such intended marriage.'[16]

This represented a considerable increase in the powers of the sovereign. The Royal Marriages Act 1772 was also considerably more stringent than the legislation that applied to the rest of the population. First, parental control over the marriages of non-royals only applied to those under the age of 21. As the House of Lords pointed out, '[i]t seems indecent to the royal family to suppose that they will not be arrived at the age of discretion as soon as the lowest subject of the realm.' Secondly, parental consent was far from absolute even in relation to those under the age of 21: minors who married after the reading of banns in their parish church did not require positive parental *consent*, though a parent could prevent the marriage from going ahead by voicing active *dissent*. And while people marrying by licence under the age of 21 without parental consent did risk having their marriage annulled at a later date, if the marriage had lasted for any reasonable period of time the courts tended to conclude that the parents must have approved of the marriage after the event and held that this was sufficient.[17] By contrast, the Royal Marriages Act made it clear that the prior consent of the sovereign had to be actively obtained, and nothing short of this would suffice. Thirdly, it was possible for non-royals to escape the provisions of the general law by eloping to another jurisdiction. But, given that the Royal Marriages Act was clear that a member of the royal family would be incapable of contracting matrimony without the prior consent of the sovereign, it followed that this was the case wherever they tried to marry.[18]

The Royal Marriages Act also imposed penalties on anybody who 'knowingly and wilfully' purported to solemnise a marriage that did not comply, or who simply attended the marriage. Again, this was not unprecedented: the Church's canon law had stipulated that those who attended a clandestine marriage would be excommunicated, while the celebrant risked suspension for three years. But the Royal Marriages Act went further in providing that those attending a ceremony that flouted its provisions would, if convicted, 'incur and suffer the penalties ordained and provided by the Statute of Provision and Praemunire.'[19] These, while less draconian than the penalties for high treason imposed for those marrying against the wishes of the sovereign in the time of Henry VIII, were still comprehensive, being 'the forfeiture of all the property, real and personal, of the person convicted for life or perpetual outlawry.'[20]

The application of the Royal Marriages Act: its scope in 1772

There was one important limitation on the scope of the Act: the issue of princesses who had married, or later married, into foreign families were not required to comply with its provisions. This immediately exempted the descendants of any of the daughters of King George II: Anne, Mary and Louise (George III's aunts) had all married into foreign families. Also exempt were the descendants of any of George III's own sisters.

His eldest, Augusta, had married the Duke of Brunswick-Wolfenbuttel several years earlier, although she apparently approved of the Act and treated her own children as subject to it.[21] Similarly, the youngest of George's siblings, Caroline Matilda, had been married to Christian VII of Denmark in 1766, when she was just fifteen.[22] The year 1772 had, however, seen her disgrace and divorce on the basis of her adultery and her departure from Denmark. In principle she would have been free to remarry, but in practice this was an unlikely prospect, especially given her subsequent residence in a castle in Hanover described as 'hard to leave and impossible to hide strangers in.'[23] So, given the exemption that applied to princesses who had married into foreign families and the prior deaths of others to whom the Act would have applied, at the time of its passage in 1772 the only unmarried adult to whom the Royal Marriages Act did apply was George III's elderly aunt Amelia (who was, at 61, unlikely to embark on matrimony and even less likely to produce children).

The impact of the Act on King George III's children

It was in the next generation that the Royal Marriages Act was to have its most dramatic impact. George III had more legitimate children than any other British monarch, but by the end of 1817, a generation after the passage of the Act, it was estimated that he had 56 illegitimate grandchildren, and not one who was legitimate.[24] His only legitimate granddaughter, Charlotte, had died in childbirth, while Frederica, the first legitimate child of his son Ernest, born in January 1817, had been stillborn.

There were obvious difficulties in finding suitable royal matches for seven princes and six princesses, but the children of George III were triply unfortunate: first, in having a father who wished his children to marry for dynastic, rather than romantic reasons; second, in that illness prevented him from fulfilling his promise to take his daughters to Hanover and allow them to choose husbands from a selected line-up of German princes, and, third, in that many of them came of marriageable age at the time of the Napoleonic wars, when Continental travel to secure possible matches with foreign royals was of necessity limited.[25] The children of George III also seem to have had a propensity for unsuitable partners. Several of his sons entered into long-term liaisons with women who would have been deemed entirely unsuitable as royal consorts at the time. Edward, Duke of Kent, had a child by Adelaide Dubus and a long-term liaison with Mademoiselle de St. Laurent, while William, Duke of Clarence, set up home with the actress Dorothy Jordan and fathered an illegitimate family of ten.[26] The Duke of York, being separated from his wife, had a rather more short-lived affair with Mary Anne Clarke which came to an abrupt end when it was discovered that she was making a living out of selling royal patronage.[27]

Such liaisons cannot be attributed solely to the harshness of the Royal Marriages Act—there were, after all, many members of the Georgian aristocracy who entered into long-term relationships with women whom they were free to marry but whose lowly social status made them undesirable as legal wives.[28] But it is possible that the near impossibility of the King consenting to a marriage with anybody not of royal blood may have led the princes to go to the opposite extreme and simply follow their hearts (or other parts of their anatomy).

Other of George III's sons married in contravention of the Royal Marriages Act. In the case of the eldest, also a George, the Act did arguably have one beneficial effect. In 1784 Prince George had fallen in love with a Catholic widow, Maria Fitzherbert. She, however, refused to succumb to his advances. Prince George proceeded to stab himself and inveigled Maria into a promise of marriage as he lay, pale and blood-stained, on his bed.[29] The following year the two went through a ceremony of marriage, though of course without the King's consent it remained void under the Royal

Marriages Act.[30] Had the marriage been valid, Prince George would have forfeited his place in the succession on account of the Act of Settlement, Maria being a Catholic. Since the marriage was not valid under the Royal Marriages Act, Prince George was not married to a Catholic in the eyes of the law and was therefore free to go through a valid marriage with his cousin, Princess Caroline of Brunswick, some years later, and to ascend the throne as King George IV in due course.

Had the Royal Marriages Act never been passed, Prince George's marriage to Maria Fitzherbert would have been valid, though George would have forfeited his personal right to succeed to the throne on account of her Catholicism.[31] Any children of their marriage, assuming that they did not adopt their mother's faith, would have been entitled to succeed. It is impossible now to speculate how legal validity might have affected the course of their relationship, but it could conceivably have led to a different line of succession right down to the present day.

Another of George III's sons Augustus (later to become the Duke of Sussex) went through no fewer than three ceremonies of marriage in contravention of the Royal Marriages Act, though to be fair two of those ceremonies involved the same woman, Lady Augusta Murray. The couple had met and married in Rome in 1793. The match seems an unlikely one: Augusta was ten years older than her prince, one biographer has described her as 'plain and rather bossy',[32] and others have noted that 'if her traducers can be believed, she was not of unblemished reputation.'[33] Contemporaries, however, were more flattering. The *Liverpool Times* described her as 'a lady of irreproachable character', and a nineteenth-century commentator claimed that at the time of the marriage 'her personal attractions were then as universally acknowledged as her many virtues and amiable qualities were beloved and esteemed to the latest period of her existence.'[34] Their marriage would not have been valid according to local law, being celebrated by a clergyman of the Church of England rather than a Roman

Catholic priest (there were, however, other contemporary cases in which the English courts upheld marriages celebrated overseas, so long as an Anglican clergyman had conducted the ceremony).[35] To be on the safe side the couple went through an Anglican ceremony upon their return to England, although yet again without the crucial element of the King's consent. Their son, Augustus, was born on January 13th, 1794, the first grandchild of George III with any claim to legitimacy. But the King refused to recognize a marriage to which he had not consented, and ordered that proceedings be set in train to have the marriage set aside.[36] The judge held that there was not sufficient evidence that any marriage had taken place in Rome, and that even if it had, it would be void. Protests that the Royal Marriages Act did not apply to marriages overseas were disregarded,[37] and Prince Augustus agreed to separate from his wife. So much for the promises he had made to her in Rome 'to love and to cherish till death us do part; to love but thee only, and none other; and may God forget me if I ever forget thee.'[38] A meeting between Augustus and Augusta in Berlin resulted in the birth of a daughter named (almost inevitably, one feels) Augusta,[39] but the reconciliation proved brief.[40] Yet in one respect Augustus, by now the Duke of Sussex, did keep his promise to Augusta—he did not remarry within her lifetime.

Meanwhile, in the absence of suitable suitors, George III's daughters pined for husbands and children. Indeed, the Princess Sophia apparently gave birth to an illegitimate child; the father was widely believed to be General Thomas Garth, the King's equerry, but disturbing rumours abounded that the child was actually the product of an incestuous union with her brother the Duke of Cumberland.[41]

As their father's health grew increasingly frail, the children of George III looked forward to such time as their brother George, Prince of Wales, might reign—either as king or regent—assuming that, given his own chequered matrimonial history, he might be more sympathetic to their choices.

Toward the end of George III's reign there was, as expected, a rush to the altar. By 1811, the King was in no position to exercise control over the marriages of his children, being scarcely able to control his own person. Responsibility for giving consent under the Royal Marriages Act thus passed to his son, Prince George, who gave consent for more marriages to take place during his nine-year tenure as Regent than his father had done in the previous forty.

One of the marriages that the Prince Regent authorized was that of his own daughter Charlotte, the sole offspring of his ill-fated marriage to Princess Caroline. Charlotte had been engaged to one prince, and entertained a fancy for another, but eventually married Prince Leopold of Saxe-Coburg. Had George III still been able to govern the marriages of his children, one doubts he would have given consent for his son Ernest, Duke of Cumberland, to marry his cousin Frederica, who was already twice married (one had ended in death, the other divorce). The King had, admittedly, earlier given consent for another son, Adolphus, to marry that same Frederica, but her jilting of Adolphus in favour of the Prince of Solms—who later divorced her[42]—might be thought to have rendered her less suitable as a royal spouse.

The King might also have taken the view that his daughters were not allying themselves with men of suitable rank. The 40-year-old Princess Mary finally married the Duke of Gloucester in 1816: though he was descended from George II, the Duke bore no royal title until his marriage.[43] And when Princess Elizabeth, at 48, wed the Hereditary Prince of Hesse Homburg, Napoleon commented contemptuously that the English royal family were 'lowering themselves... with little petty princes.'[44] When their sister Augusta wished to marry a mere 'Sir', however, it appears that consent was not forthcoming even from the Prince Regent: whether she went ahead regardless and married the man of her choice, Major General Sir Brent Spencer, remains a mystery.[45]

Had he been *compos mentis*, George III would probably have looked with more favour upon the weddings of his sons the Dukes of Clarence, Kent, and Cambridge, who all married foreign princesses within weeks of each other. The timing was no coincidence: after the death of the Prince Regent's daughter Princess Charlotte in 1817, the race was on to provide a legitimate heir to the throne. The jilted Adolphus, Duke of Cambridge, married Princess Augusta of Hesse-Cassel, their son being born in March of 1819, while the Dukes of Clarence and Kent both callously cast off their long-term lovers in order to make suitable matches.[46]

But there was one final marriage of which George III would definitely have disapproved. After the death of Lady Augusta Murray in 1830, the Duke of Sussex went through a ceremony of marriage with Lady Cecilia Buggin.[47] Once again consent for the match under the Royal Marriages Act was neither sought nor given, and the marriage was on that account void.

Despite this late flurry of marriages, it is clear that the 1772 Act had a profound impact upon the lives of George III's children. As noted above, if Prince George's marriage to Maria Fitzherbert been valid they would in all likelihood have produced heirs to the throne. In the event, of course, it was the Duke of Clarence who went on to reign as King William IV, but—despite having provided ample proof of his fertility in the illegitimate children he had sired—he also died without a legitimate heir. The crown therefore passed to the Duke of Kent's teenage daughter, Victoria, who was to set a very different example from that of her dissolute uncles.

The next generation

Queen Victoria appears to have had more sympathy than her grandfather for those affected by the provisions of his Royal Marriages Act. She even went so far as to confer the title of Duchess of Inverness upon Lady Cecilia Buggin, the second non-wife of her uncle the Duke of Sussex, as a reward for their siding with her on a separate issue of royal precedence.[48] And, when her cousin George, son of the Duke of Cambridge, went through a ceremony of marriage with the actress Louisa Fairbrother in 1847,[49] the couple were subsequently accepted at court. Although their marriage was clearly void—the consent of the Queen had not been sought, presumably to save her the embarrassment of having to refuse it—it was never formally challenged and proved to be both happy and enduring.

But Victoria also appeared to relish the power that the Royal Marriages Act conferred upon her. Her consent was not only necessary for the marriages of those members of the royal family resident in England, but also for the marriages of the royal family of Hanover. The two had been united by the same ruler since 1714, but, since the law of Hanover did not allow for a female sovereign, in 1837 the crown had passed to Victoria's uncle the Duke of Cumberland as King Ernest I. While the Royal Marriages Act specifically exempted the issue of princesses who married into foreign families, it was silent as to the approach to be taken over the issue of princes who ruled over foreign countries: King Ernest and his descendants continued to bear the titles of British royalty in addition to their Hanoverian titles.

Accordingly, in 1880 Ernest's granddaughter Frederica came to England to ask Victoria's consent for her marriage to the Baron de Rammingen. The twist in the tale was that Frederica's brother, the King of Hanover, had refused his consent—but Victoria grandly reminded him that *she* was the head of the family, and gave her consent to the marriage. Frederica was 'a British subject and English Princess and as such, if she has the consent of the Sovereign she can marry anyone whom she will.'[50] Specific legislation was passed declaring that Luitbert Alexander George Lionel Alphons Freiherr von Pawel-Rammingen was a British subject,[51] and he married Frederica in St George's Chapel on April 24th.

But even if their marriage had taken place in Hanover, the parties would still have needed to comply with the

Royal Marriages Act, for the Act's application to marriages conducted overseas had been confirmed some years earlier. The question had arisen after the death of the Duke of Sussex in 1843, whereupon his son Augustus had petitioned the Queen for the right to assume his father's titles. Of course, his parents' marriage in Rome had already been declared void in the church courts on account of its flouting the Act, but English law at the time dealt with different aspects of the law of marriage in different courts, and there was a possibility that a secular court might decide that there was sufficient evidence of a ceremony of marriage to entitle Augustus to what he claimed.

At this time the church courts still had power to decide whether a marriage itself was *valid* or not[52] (though they were to lose this jurisdiction to the secular courts in 1857), but other courts might be required to decide on issues that rested on the *existence* of a marriage—for example whether a particular woman was a wife for the purposes of inheritance or property ownership.[53] It was a subtle but vital distinction. In some legal contexts the fact that a ceremony had taken place would be sufficient to establish certain rights, regardless of whether or not the marriage would have been upheld as valid by the church courts.

So there was nothing odd in the House of Lords devoting several days to a discussion of whether the younger Augustus was in fact entitled to assume the titles he claimed; it was, nonetheless, unsurprising that they should come to the conclusion that he was not. A panel of judges advised their Lordships that, since Augustus' father had been 'precisely within the class... of persons' governed by the Royal Marriages Act, there was no possibility of his evading its effect by marrying abroad. After pages of impassioned rhetoric by Augustus' counsel, their Lordships delivered brief speeches to the effect that although the ceremony had taken place, it was clearly invalid under the Royal Marriages Act and therefore had no legal consequences at all.

Their conclusion was supported by reference to the purpose of the legislation and the very fact that it made provision for notice to be given to the Privy Council should consent be refused.

> 'it is scarcely supposable that the Legislature should have provided the minute and laborious machinery of the second section... if the party himself who is the subject of such legislation, by an easy journey, or a voyage of a few hours, could render all these provisions useless, and set the statute at defiance.'[54]

In other words, what was the point of having a Royal Marriages Act, if royals could simply hop on a boat to Calais or a stage-coach to Scotland to enter into a valid marriage without the monarch's consent?

From one perspective, the *Sussex Peerage Case* was of little importance, simply confirming the earlier decision of the church courts over the marriage of the Duke of Sussex in 1794. But the very fact that the territorial scope of the Royal Marriages Act had been decided at the highest level was in itself of significance. Decisions of the House of Lords were binding, not only on the lower courts but even on itself. The case also made it clear that the legal establishment were willing to give their backing to the Royal Marriages Act, despite the criticisms that had been levelled at it by the wider public. The earlier decision of the church courts could have been seen as motivated by deference to a slighted monarch; the decision of the House of Lords, by contrast, confirmed as a matter of legal principle that the Royal Marriages Act applied wherever in the world the ceremony took place.

And the case had far wider implications for the marriages of other descendants of George II. Members of the Hanover family continued to request the consent of the British monarch to their marriages.[55] But the possibility of the Act invalidating other overseas royal marriages was to become a very real one as a result of developments in the twentieth century.

The challenges of the twentieth century

Throughout the nineteenth century the convention that members of the British royal family marry foreign princes and princesses had largely been maintained. The fact that a mere marquis was deemed a suitable husband for Queen Victoria's daughter Louise in 1871 is best attributed to the aging Queen's desire to keep her family close—rather than having her daughters marrying into foreign royal families[56]—and not to any change in the importance attached to a spouse's status.

Change came about for pragmatic reasons rather than under the influence of any new romantic ideas about marrying for love, and it was the First World War that provided the catalyst. At a time when Britain was at war with Germany, it was seen as politic to announce that the tradition of marrying members of other—and by definition foreign—royal families would cease. King George V wrote in his diary that he had informed the Privy Council how 'May[57] and I decided some time ago that our children would be allowed to marry into British families,' adding, with characteristic understatement, 'it was quite a historical occasion.'[58] At the same time the Germanic surname Battenburg was anglicized to Mountbatten, and the defiantly English Windsor was substituted for Saxe-Coburg-Gotha. As David Starkey notes, the monarchy was simultaneously 'anglicized and humanized'.[59] In consultation with the Prime Minister[60] it was further agreed that royal titles would be limited to the monarch, his children and grandchildren.[61]

And once the war was over there were further compelling reasons for not limiting one's choice of spouse to other royals. There were, quite simply, far fewer royal families in 1918 than there had been in 1914. The Romanovs had been murdered, the Hapsburg empire destroyed, the German imperial throne had fallen and the rulers of assorted kingdoms, dukedoms and principalities had been required to abdicate. Many of the remaining houses looked to be under threat from republican movements.[62] By the end of the First World War, Europe's several dozen royal houses had been whittled down to just fifteen, of which a mere four were Protestant. Had the British royal family looked for spouses only among the unmarried adult princes and princesses of Europe's Protestant royalty, their choice would have been limited indeed.[63]

Significantly, it was at this stage that royal weddings began to be grand public affairs, despite, or perhaps because of, the fact that royalty were now marrying minor aristocracy or even commoners rather than the rapidly diminishing stock of foreign royals. In 1839, Westminster Abbey had been rejected as a venue for the marriage of Queen Victoria to Prince Albert on the basis that it would be 'like a second Coronation.'[64] Eighty years later, however, it was the chosen location for the wedding of Victoria's granddaughter Princess Patricia of Connaught to Commander the Honourable Alexander Ramsay on February 27th, 1919. But Princess Patricia's wedding attracted a large and enthusiastic crowd and set the ball rolling for future royal events. Three years later Princess Mary, the only daughter of King George V, married Viscount Lascelles there in a celebration 'acclaimed... as the most spectacular royal event since the King's coronation in 1911.'[65] And on April 26th, 1923, the Abbey was the location for the marriage of the future King George VI to Lady Elizabeth Bowes-Lyon.[66]

Indeed, since 1917, only two members of the royal family have married other royalty—the Duke of Kent, who married Princess Marina of Greece in 1934, and the present Queen. This has raised a new problem. The Royal Marriages Act was drafted on the assumption that princesses would marry into foreign royal houses and no longer be subject to its terms. Setting aside for the moment exactly when this exemption applies—itself a matter of some debate—the fact that twentieth-century princesses were marrying British subjects has meant that their descendants have remained subject to the requirements of the Act.

As the years passed and the number of descendants of George II subject to the Act multiplied, there were those who grumbled about its application. In 1949 the Earl of Harewood, the son of Princess Mary and Viscount Lascelles, found to his dismay that his intended marriage to the Austrian pianist Marion Stein was not greeted with enthusiasm. King George VI initially refused to consent to his nephew's marriage, not because he disapproved of the match but because his mother did. Lord Harewood noted ruefully in his autobiography that his uncle 'refused to give me his permission until Queen Mary had agreed. He implied that that would take a little time.'[67] Queen Mary, who had been engaged to one future king and married another,[68] was always likely to attach more weight than most to the claims of status. Still, she eventually relented after a conversation with her grandson, and the marriage went ahead.

In the meantime, however, more serious questions had arisen over the operation of the Royal Marriages Act—or, rather, over a crucial omission in its drafting.

Marriage and the monarch

One objection to the Act that had been raised at the time of its passage was that it did not apply to a reigning monarch. This was far from being a minor oversight, as it left the most important personage in the kingdom free to marry whomsoever they chose without regard for the dynastic consequences. George III had himself been unmarried when he succeeded to the throne in 1760, although by the time of his coronation in 1761 he had wed Charlotte of Mecklenburg-Strelitz.[69] His granddaughter Victoria found herself similarly unconstrained in her choice of spouse when she became Queen in 1837, simply announcing her intended choice to her ministers.[70] But she had informed her Prime Minister,

Lord Melbourne, before she actually proposed to Albert, and clearly had his approval for her choice.[71] And her journals and letters show that she was keenly aware that her marriage was not merely a personal matter, but one in which the country as a whole had a legitimate interest.[72]

But what if a reigning monarch wished to marry someone deemed to be 'unsuitable'? Such was the issue that faced ministers in 1936. In the wake of the death of King George V, his eldest son, who had succeeded to the throne as Edward VIII, declared his intention to marry Wallis Simpson once she had obtained a divorce from her second husband. Under the terms of the Royal Marriages Act, Edward, as King, had no need of consent from anyone. But Sir Donald Somervell, the Attorney-General, pointed out that although the Royal Marriages Act did not apply to a reigning monarch, it would be unconstitutional for the reigning monarch to marry against the advice of ministers.[73] This did not mean that such a marriage would not be valid. But it did mean that a monarch who persisted in his choice might face the resignation of his entire government—or be led to believe that his own abdication was necessary.

The abdication crisis has been subjected to more academic and popular discussion than any other royal event of the twentieth century, and I do not intend to engage in detailed discussion here, since the points of interest it raises relate to the law of divorce rather than the law of marriage.[74] It would appear that there were a number of different reasons for different individuals to oppose the match: for some it was the fact that Wallis was American, for others it was the fact that she had already had two husbands.[75] Members of the royal family seem to have been concerned that her influence on Edward was not beneficial.[76] Others were concerned about her—and his—political sympathies, which leant towards support for Hitler's Germany. The suggestion of a morganatic marriage (that is, one in which none of Edward's titles or ranks would pass to his wife or their children) was firmly rejected by the Cabinet and by the Prime Ministers of the Dominions.[77] The crucial point for present purposes is that, as the constitutional historian Vernon Bogdanor has highlighted, the crisis established that the monarch's choice of a spouse *was* limited[78]—and that the duty of a king to act in accordance with the advice of his ministers or risk a constitutional crisis might be as powerful in this respect as statute law.

Once Edward had decided that he would give up his throne rather than his love for Mrs Simpson, it was necessary for Parliament to pass specific legislation to bring this about. This momentous change was effected by a very short and simple statute. His Majesty's Declaration of Abdication Act, passed on December 11th, 1936, was barely longer than its title, but it did three important things: it provided that Edward would cease to be King, and that the succession would pass to the next in line; it stipulated that neither Edward nor his descendants would have any future claim to the throne; and it specifically provided that the Royal Marriages Act would not apply to Edward after his abdication.[79] This last point was vital: after all, abdication would not otherwise alter the fact that Edward was a descendant of George II, and as such subject to the Royal Marriages Act. There could have been no question of his younger brother, once he had become King George VI, assenting to a marriage that had proved so controversial and had led to an abdication. On the other hand, it would have been too ironic if Edward had been unable to enter into the marriage he had sacrificed his throne for, and so specific legislation was needed to disapply the Royal Marriages Act.

The marriage of the (by-then) Duke of Windsor to Wallis Simpson eventually[80] took place in a French chateau, the civil ceremony required under French law being followed by a (legally superfluous) Anglican service—a far cry from his younger brothers' weddings at Westminster Abbey. Members of the royal family were invited to attend, but none chose to do so.[81]

What the Abdication Act of 1936 does show, of course, is that passing specific legislation to disapply the effect of the Royal Marriages Act was possible. And that possibility was to be discussed again before very long.

The princess and the pilot

The abdication crisis had confirmed the limitations that hedged any monarch. And, just as constitutional convention required that ministers be consulted not only about the sovereign's own choice of spouse, the same was true of the giving of consent under the Royal Marriages Act. Such consultation was 'admittedly somewhat perfunctory'[82] in the case of the marriage of the heir-presumptive Princess Elizabeth to Prince Philip in 1947, the suitability of the match being beyond question. But five years later the new Queen Elizabeth was to face the more difficult question of whether to give her consent to a marriage between her sister and her late father's former equerry, Group-Captain Peter Townsend.

The familiarity of the story of the frustrated romance between Princess Margaret and the divorced Townsend should not be allowed to obscure the importance of the issues being discussed. As Townsend himself later noted, the Queen was in a delicate position in that she 'was Head of the State, which permitted divorce' but also 'Head of the State Church, which did not.'[83] File after file in the National Archives is filled with anxious discussion of how to deal with the situation, their covers barely visible under labels reading 'SECRET' and, occasionally, 'TOP SECRET'. The public profile of Princess Margaret meant that the possibility of a quiet wedding in defiance of the Act was simply not an option. For the first time, therefore, it was necessary for the authorities to contemplate how a member of the royal family might validly marry without the sovereign's consent.

The differences between Margaret's case and that of her uncle Edward were more striking than the similarities.

Whether a divorce should actually have been granted to Wallis Simpson on the basis of her then husband Ernest's adultery was a very moot point: at the time, both collusion and the petitioner's own adultery had the potential to bar the granting of a divorce, and research has shown that 'material evidence in official hands was not in fact considered.'[84] By contrast, no such issues seem to have arisen in relation to Townsend's divorce from his first wife Rosemary, who had remarried only a month after the decree absolute.[85] Public attitudes had also changed. Divorce had become more freely available in the intervening years (the Matrimonial Causes Act 1937 had allowed divorce on the basis of cruelty and desertion, in addition to adultery), and the numbers taking advantage of this option had increased, especially in the wake of the War. There was considerable public support for Margaret to marry Townsend. A poll in the *Daily Mirror* elicited over 70,000 responses, 97 per cent of which were in favour of the marriage.[86] Finally, of course, the marriage was of lesser constitutional significance. Margaret had already slipped down to third place in the line of succession in the wake of the birth of the Queen's first two children. Those who had baulked at the idea of a twice-divorced American becoming queen might well have been willing to accept a dashing and highly decorated fighter pilot as the husband of a princess.

But the abdication crisis did, nonetheless, loom over the romance between Margaret and Townsend. If consent could now be given to Margaret to marry a divorced man, why had Edward VIII given up his crown to marry the woman he loved? In the run-up to the coronation of Elizabeth II in 1953, it was clearly undesirable to take any step that might expose the monarchy to criticism.[87] Townsend left the royal household for a post in Brussels, and Margaret continued to carry out such royal duties as were allotted to the sister of a queen.

Less than a year later, however, it was made clear that the Queen did have the power to consent to a marriage even if one of the parties had been divorced. Captain Ramsay—son of Princess Patricia who in 1919 had set the trend for royal weddings at Westminster Abbey—wished to marry a divorcee.[88] A memorandum from the Lord Chancellor's Office in March 1954 expressed the view that the Queen could give her consent to this marriage without even taking the advice of her ministers. One reason for this was the view that a refusal would attract more attention than the giving of consent: if consent were to be refused, and Captain Ramsay were to pursue the matter by giving notice to the Privy Council, 'there would be at least a serious risk of some busybody taking the matter up in either House of Parliament.'[89] The giving of consent, by contrast, would attract little attention: the Captain was extremely remote from the succession and did not bear any royal title. It was emphasised that this case created no 'awkward precedent' and that a different approach might need to be taken for those closer to the throne.[90]

And the caution of government advisers on this point was understandable, for the thorny issue of Margaret's possible marriage to Townsend had merely been put off, rather than resolved. As she approached the age of twenty-five during the summer of 1955, there was renewed speculation as to her matrimonial intentions.[91]

The significance of this birthday was that the provisions of the Royal Marriages Act allowed those attaining that age to marry against the sovereign's wishes,[92] although a long drawn-out procedure had to be followed. Any member of the royal family wishing to marry without the sovereign's consent had to give notice to the Privy Council, as the memorandum relating to Captain Ramsay had noted. They then had to wait a further twelve months. If no objections were made, the marriage could go ahead, but it was still within the power of Parliament to prevent the marriage by expressly declaring its disapprobation.[93]

When the giving of consent had lain in the personal power

of the monarch, the process of giving notice to the Privy Council had provided a potential appeal against unreasonable refusals. But if royal consent was only to be reasonably withheld after consultation with ministers, further questions arose. Would ministers who had advised the monarch to withhold consent from a particular marriage go on to initiate a motion challenging that marriage in Parliament, and thereby potentially prevent it from going ahead?

Advisors in the Lord Chancellor's Office took the view that this was highly unlikely in this particular case. The assumption underpinning their discussions was that there were marriages to which the monarch should not be *seen* to consent, but which should nonetheless be allowed to go ahead. Indeed, the concern of advisers was that some inconsiderate MP might actually try to object to the marriage by initiating a motion to prevent it. Could the government in such a case, it was wondered, publicly put the whips on to defeat such a motion, given that this would be directly at odds with their advice to the monarch to refuse consent? Such issues all had to be given serious consideration, but the view was taken that it was very unlikely that any such motion would be made 'in any but an extreme case outside reasonable contemplation.' Even if such a motion were made, it was thought that it would not secure a majority in its favour but would be 'defeated by the good feeling and good taste of the House.'[94] Lord Kilmuir, the Lord Chancellor, concurred that it was probable that there would be no motion in either House, but acknowledged that a motion in the Commons—presumably less to be relied upon for 'good feeling and good taste'—was at least 'possible'.

In short, a marriage without the consent of the monarch was possible in Margaret's case, and only in the unlikely event of both houses of Parliament passing a motion objecting to the marriage could it be prevented once she had reached the stipulated age. There was, however, an alternative option being canvassed, and here the abdication crisis, rather than being part of the problem, actually provided a solution, if a drastic one. The Declaration of Abdication Act had, as we have seen, specifically excluded the former Edward VIII from the operation of the Royal Marriages Act and so allowed him to marry without the consent of his successor. And so it was suggested that, where a member of the royal family wished to contract a marriage to which the monarch would not consent, it would be possible to do so 'by signing a declaration of abdication of all rights to the succession.'[95] Legislation would then be necessary to confirm this and—as in the case of Edward—to provide that the Royal Marriages Act would no longer apply to that individual.

A third way of escaping the issue of whether the Queen should be seen to give her consent to the marriage of her sister to a divorcee was to reform the Royal Marriages Act itself. This was not a novel suggestion—reform had been proposed even before the question of Margaret's possible marriage to Townsend arose—but it had obviously acquired new urgency. The main flaw of the Act, it was noted, was the number of persons to whom it might potentially apply. It was suggested that it should be limited to the children and grandchildren of the sovereign,[96] and the heir-presumptive. This would be wide enough to exercise control over the marriages of those likely to inherit the throne, but narrow enough to exclude Princess Margaret.

But although the Lord Chancellor favoured this option, the Law Officers of the Crown, feeling that the proposed circle was too narrow, did not. The Law Officers (i.e., the Attorney-General and the Solicitor-General) also took the view that the consequences of marrying without the monarch's consent should be altered: rather than such a marriage being invalid, they thought that the sanction should be 'automatic exclusion from the Throne and forfeiture of any Civil List income.' Realising that any such alteration in the law would require careful thought and drafting, their suggested method of dealing with the immediate issue was to pass legislation dealing only with Princess Margaret herself, and to pursue the question of more wide-ranging reform 'in consultation with the Dominions.'

Reference to the Dominions highlights yet another complicating factor. Under the terms of the Statute of Westminster of 1931, any alteration in the law 'touching the succession to the Throne' would require the assent of the Parliaments of the all the Dominions. And this was thought to apply not only to any specific legislation whereby Margaret might renounce her right to the throne, but also to any amendment to the Royal Marriages Act.[97]

But the difficulties of passing legislation—whether general or specific—to enable Margaret to marry Townsend should not obscure the fact that legislation was not the only option. As late as June 1955 government advisers were discussing the possibility of Margaret giving notice to the Privy Council—and so invoking the machinery of the Royal Marriages Act to bring about a marriage against the monarch's wishes—as an alternative to giving up her title and place in the succession. And, given that such a marriage would *not* alter the succession, there was no reason why the assent of the Dominion Parliaments should be required for it to take place.

The puzzle then is why discussion of the simple (if lengthy) option of giving notice to the Privy Council seems to have been quietly dropped. By late 1955 the issue was being presented as a stark choice between love and status. According to Townsend, when Anthony Eden, the Prime Minister, met with Margaret on October 1st, he warned her that marriage 'would bring her the most grievous penalties: she would have to renounce her royal rights, functions and income.'[98] Townsend noted sadly that this was the first time that the consequences had been made clear to them. But the route laid down by the Royal Marriages Act did *not* require an individual to give up their royal status or their place in the succession, a point easily missed in the welter of different alternatives being canvassed behind the scenes. At some point there must have been a deliberate decision to obfuscate this option.

The files of the memoranda that flew back and forth between different government departments in early October and the drafts and redrafts of announcements for different contingencies illustrate the genuine uncertainty regarding Margaret's intentions. Government officials even drafted a statement for Margaret in the event of her deciding to marry Townsend, to the effect that 'it is her wish to renounce her rights of succession to the Throne, on behalf of herself and her children.'[99] It seems to have been the leading article in *The Times* on October 26th that finally tipped the balance. Margaret's marriage to a divorced man would, it proclaimed, damage the monarchy, and would prevent her from playing any further role as a member of the royal family. The leader-writer then struck a more plaintive note: what, it demanded, would the Queen do without the support of her sister? Margaret's renunciation of royal status would leave the Queen 'still more lonely in her arduous life of public service in which she needs the support and cooperation that only her close kindred can give.'

In the light of such manipulation, it was of no consequence that many of the arguments in the editorial were, as Townsend dryly noted, 'specious', or that other papers spoke out in favour of the match.[100] After reading it, Townsend himself sat down and wrote out a speech for Margaret to deliver. Margaret's message to the press laid stress on the fact that she had come to this decision by herself. But would she, one wonders, have decided not to marry Townsend if the full range of options and their consequences had been made clear to her?

An unexpectedly British prince, a very British solution

With Margaret's announcement that she would not after all be marrying Townsend, it might have seemed that the immediate necessity for reform of the Royal Marriages Act had passed. But even while the debate as to Margaret's possible marriage was taking place, events were already underway that were to present a new set of unanticipated problems with the Act. And this time, the issue related to the scope of the Act itself.

There had not long before been suggestions that the Act no longer applied to the key members of the British royal family, the argument focusing on the implications of the exemption for princesses marrying into foreign families. Writing in 1951, the barrister and academic Charles Farran had put forward the ingenious thesis that the Act no longer applied to *any* of the descendants of Edward VII on the basis that they were, as a result of cross-marriages, the issue of a princess who had married into a foreign family.[101] The background facts were clear: in 1863, Edward VII (then Prince of Wales) had married Princess Alexandra of Denmark. She herself was a descendant of George II through his daughter Princess Louise, who had married the King of Denmark in 1743.[102] As the issue of a princess who had married into a foreign family, Louise's descendants would be exempt from compliance with the Royal Marriages Act. All were agreed on this. What was disputed was Farran's contention was that this exemption was unaffected by the fact that Louise's great-great-granddaughter Alexandra had married *back* into the British royal family.

Farran's article was widely disseminated and discussed in Whitehall, but its readers were generally unconvinced.[103] In effect, marriage back into the British royal family was thought to override any exemption resulting from one's descent, although official files do not contain any clear and cogent reasoning on this point.[104] But the issue of cross-marriages was crucial to a very different, and far more problematic, interpretation of the Act. What if those who had assumed they were marrying into *foreign* families had in fact married *British* subjects? Would their issue still be exempted from the need to comply with the Royal Marriages Act? And if they were not exempt, just how many marriages might be invalid for lack of the necessary royal consent?

The reason this argument came to the fore at this particular time is a legal challenge brought by the German Prince Ernest of Hanover. Prince Ernest wished to claim British nationality under the terms of the Princess Sophia Naturalization Act of 1705.[105] This had provided, in the wake of the Act of Settlement four years earlier, that Princess Sophia and all her lineal descendants 'born or hereafter to be born' would be regarded in law as 'natural-born subjects' of England and Wales. While this might appear clear, the preamble to the Act had also referred to the importance of Princess Sophia and her descendants becoming naturalised during the lifetime of Queen Anne. The question before the court was whether this limited the effect of the Act solely to the twelve descendants of Princess Sophia born before Queen Anne's death in 1714—or whether *all* descendants of Princess Sophia in the intervening 250 years had been, and still were, entitled to British nationality.[106] It was decided by the House of Lords in 1957 that Prince Ernest was indeed entitled to British nationality. Viscount Simonds acknowledged that although an interpretation 'which would lead to most of the Royal families of Europe being British subjects' might well be regarded as 'absurd', the idea of British nationality being conferred on those born after Queen Anne's death was not so manifestly absurd as to be rejected.[107]

So, if Prince Ernest of Hanover was entitled to British nationality, then the same was true of countless other descendants of Princess Sophia. The precise numbers were disputed: it was suggested that by the mid-1950s around 400 individuals might have unexpectedly and unknowingly acquired British nationality as a result of the decision, but one genealogically-minded member of the public put the figure at over 1,200.[108] The implications were also disputed: the Lord Chancellor preferred the comforting view that a princess could be regarded as having married into a foreign family even if her spouse was, unbeknownst to her, also a British national. But the Law Officers, rather inconveniently, took the contrary view.

When combined with the number of cross-marriages

that had occurred over the previous two centuries[109] and the principle laid down over a century earlier by the *Sussex Peerage Case*, the results were potentially explosive. As Farran had pointed out:

> '[i]t is at least arguable that the terms of the Royal Marriages Act are so categoric that even a foreign-domiciled person—if he is not within the exemptive words—must be treated by the English courts as being incapable of matrimony without the British King's consent.'

In other words, the Act, if read literally, required *anybody* who could trace his or her legitimate genealogy back to George II to have the consent of the British monarch to marry, unless the exemption for princesses marrying into foreign families applied. And, of course, the case of Prince Ernest had just demonstrated that the number of those exempted might be far, far smaller than had been assumed.

If this were right, the consequences would be extremely embarrassing. Behind the scenes, it was noted anxiously that among those whose parents' marriages would be invalidated under the Royal Marriages Act would be Lord Mountbatten, the second Marquess of Milford Haven, the Queen of Sweden, and Princess Andrew of Greece;[110] and since no consent had been given to the marriage of Princess Andrew of Greece either, then her son—Prince Philip, the Duke of Edinburgh—would also be illegitimate.[111]

Three options to deal with the problem were considered in a secret memorandum from the Attorney-General, Reginald Manningham-Buller, in March 1957.[112] The first was to legislate to remove British nationality from the persons concerned. This, he thought, would be 'tyrannous' as well as raising awkward questions about the Royal Marriages Act. The second option of legislating to confirm the validity of the marriages that had been cast into question would, however, be no less embarrassing, and 'would give further opportunities for argument on the Royal Marriages Act as well as requiring consultation with Commonwealth governments.' Less than two years after Margaret had given up the idea of marrying Townsend, this was clearly to be avoided. The third—and in his eyes best—course was 'to do nothing', unless any of the marriages in question should actually be disputed.

The new Prime Minister, Harold Macmillan, shared Manningham-Buller's view. The last piece in the relevant file is a small square of paper with the enigmatic observation that "*Quieta non movere*" was the favourite motto of one of the greatest of my predecessors.' In other words, let sleeping dogs lie. As a result, despite the arguments that, on the one hand, the Royal Marriages Act applied to virtually no members of the British royal family, and, on the other, that it might apply to many members of foreign royal families who had assumed themselves exempt, no action was taken.

Once again, the opportunity for reform of the law had not been taken up. The potentially calamitous effects of any future unwitting failure to obtain royal consent were, however, to be mitigated by a discreet clause in the Legitimacy Act of 1959.[113] This provided, amongst other things, that children of a void marriage should be treated as legitimate if their parents had been ignorant of the factor rendering the marriage void. Uniquely among legislation of this kind, it was further provided that any such child would have the same right as one born legitimate to succeed to 'dignities and titles of honour'—although not to the throne.[114]

Consent and the constitution

In addition to the uncertainty as to the scope of the Act, events that came to pass in the 1960s raised questions over the precise constitutional requirement on the sovereign regarding the giving of consent. The distinction drawn in the previous decade between the proposed marriages of Alexander Ramsay and Princess Margaret had rested on their respective closeness to the succession: the Queen had a constitutional duty to consult her ministers in the case of her sister, but not in that of a remote cousin. But come the 1960s the approach adopted seemed to rest not on whether the Queen could consent to the marriage in question, but rather on whether she should be seen to be doing so.

So, for example, when Princess Margaret herself became engaged to Anthony Armstrong-Jones in 1960, the Cabinet absolved the Queen from any duty to seek its advice before giving her consent under the Royal Marriages Act. Her only duty was to inform her ministers of any intended marriage, and then only when 'the closeness to the succession justifies that course.'[115] A further memorandum suggested that it was not for the Queen to ask for advice, but for ministers 'to decide whether they should tender it.' The wording of any advice also had to take into account the sensibilities of the other countries in the Commonwealth. As Lord Kilmuir, then Lord Chancellor, mused, 'It has never been the practice for their ministers to be asked for or to give advice, but trouble might arise if it were known that we did and they did not.'

By contrast, seven years later in 1967, a different approach was taken to the proposed remarriage of the Queen's cousin, the Earl of Harewood. Sued for adultery by his first wife Marion, he wished to marry the woman with whom he had been living, Patricia Tuckwell.[116] But he needed consent under the Royal Marriages Act in order to do so.

Given that at the time the Earl was eighteenth in line to the throne, this was clearly not a marriage that was so close to the succession as to require ministerial input in the usual run of things, and consent would under normal circumstances have been forthcoming. The problem of course was that Harewood, like Peter Townsend, was a divorcee, and so, for that matter, was Patricia. Could the Queen, as Defender of the Faith, be seen to sanction a double remarriage which would not be possible in the Church of England? There again, if she refused consent, would she be seen as obliging the couple to live together unwed? As one commentator noted, 'Harewood's behaviour had not proved a threat to the throne, but Elizabeth II's subsequent condemnation might.'[117]

The dilemma encapsulated the weakness of the Royal Marriages Act in an era that was beginning to see new challenges to marriage itself. For earlier generations, prohibiting a marriage was the same as prohibiting a relationship. But that was hardly the case here: a son, Mark, had already been born,[118] the Earl had been cohabiting with Patricia for the previous sixteen months,[119] and the refusal of consent was unlikely to change their domestic arrangements. Pointed questions were asked in Parliament. Was the Prime Minister aware, demanded one backbencher, referring to George III's Royal Marriages Act, that

> 'this outworn relic of a spiteful family feud is always liable to place the Crown in an embarrassing position of having to decide whether or not to grant permission to marry someone a long way removed from the line of succession?'[120]

The Queen indicated to the Prime Minister, Harold Wilson, that she wished to be advised by the Cabinet. He had a duty to give her the Cabinet's advice, and she had a duty to take it.[121] Neither was in any doubt as to what that advice would be, and it was carefully recorded that

> 'the Cabinet had advised the Queen to give her consent and Her Majesty has signified her intention to do so.'[122]

The official files on the Harewood affair remain closed to the public, and so one can only speculate on the discussions behind the scenes. Distinguishing his case from that of Margaret only twelve years earlier would not, however, have posed too many difficulties for advisers. The broader social changes that had occurred since 1955 made the issue much easier to resolve. Ideas about the law had changed radically even in this short period. In the mid-fifties a number of powerful figures were still advancing the idea that it was correct to use the law as an instrument of social control. By the late 1960s, though, divorce had become more frequent and considerably more acceptable, and the newly-created Law Commission was calling for the law to be reformed to enable those in 'stable illicit unions' to obtain a divorce and then regularise their new relationship in remarriage. The role of the law had become one of responding to change and minimising the hardship suffered by individuals.

At the time of his first marriage, Harewood had described the Royal Marriages Act as 'a crazy anomaly'.[123] And if it was anomalous in the mid-twentieth century, it was still more so by its close.

The Royal Marriages Act in the twenty-first century

Criticism of the Act has tended to emerge at times when consent is refused or likely to be refused. But the very lack of any refusals in recent years does also raise questions about the point of the continuing requirement to seek consent.

Given changing social mores, it is difficult to imagine the circumstances in which the Queen would now refuse consent to a marriage. At the start of her reign, the influence of the Church of England was sufficiently strong for her to feel unable to consent to the marriage of her sister to a divorcee; today, by contrast, it is often possible for divorcees to remarry in the Anglican Church. The changing attitudes to divorce and remarriage are reflected in the very different fates of Margaret in the 1950s and Harewood in the 1960s. Yet even then, it would seem, the Queen's consent was not accompanied by her blessing: Harewood 'became a "non-person" within the royal family',[124] not even receiving an invitation to Princess Anne's wedding in 1973. But come 1992 the Queen was to sanction Anne's second marriage, and a decade later gave her consent to a marriage involving two divorcees—her son Charles and Camilla Parker Bowles—although only, of course, after complying with 'her constitutional obligations to follow prime ministerial advice.'[125]

This is not to imply that the Queen should not have given her consent to such marriages. It is, rather, to point out that ideas about 'suitable' spouses have undergone a revolution since the eighteenth century and that the giving of consent is now an empty formality. Since suitability is now determined by the parties' affection for each other, it is difficult to imagine any cases in which it would be deemed appropriate for consent to be refused. Commentators have described the Act as effectively 'obsolete' in this regard.[126]

Indeed, because of the different geneses of the various rules applying to royal marriages, the consent of the monarch is required even to marriages that will have the effect of excluding the individual in question from the succession. In 2006, for example, the Queen sanctioned the marriage of Lord Nicholas Windsor to fellow-Catholic Paola Doimi de Frankopan. As one observer commented, this was 'the first time since the royal marriages act in the 18th century that a monarch had sanctioned a fully Catholic royal wedding.'[127] Nicholas' Catholicism would have been sufficient to exclude him from the succession anyway, but his marriage to Paola would have had that effect independently of his own faith.

No doubt most of those who are required to seek the Queen's consent for their marriages rather treasure this royal link. Some who technically had no need of consent have still sought it. Both Emily and Benjamin Lascelles, the oldest children of Viscount Lascelles, had the Queen's consent for their respective marriages, but since their parents were unmarried at the time of their births there was no requirement for them to do so.

In the light of the number of royal princes who in past times sired children outside marriage, one can only be thankful that the Royal Marriages Act does not apply to such issue. Only legislation passed after the Family Law Reform Act in 1987 has had to be construed without regard to the marital status of a child's parents, meaning that today illegitimacy still has the effect of severing the application of the Royal Marriages Act. This at least reduces the likelihood of marriages being invalidated when one party discovers their previously unsuspected descent from George II—which, indeed, is not a fanciful prospect: in 2008 the BBC TV programme *Who Do You Think You Are?* revealed to the politician Boris Johnson that he was in fact a descendant of King George II, albeit through an ancestor born on the wrong side of the blanket.

But there may well be others whose marriages are technically void on account of their failure to comply with the Royal Marriages Act. If, when the matter was considered in the late 1950s, there were many hundreds of descendants of George II who might unwittingly be British citizens, how many might there be today? It is not inconceivable that, where titles and wealth are concerned, a suit might one day be brought by an individual who stands to inherit if they can show that a particular marriage was void through lack of royal consent. The absurdity was summed up by one nineteenth-century lawyer:

> 'Are all the remote descendants of George II, who and whose parents may have lived abroad, away from the operation of the laws of this country, and perhaps ignorant of their existence, are they all to be subjected to the provisions of this Act, and to be incapable of marrying except with the consent of the Sovereign of this country?'[128]

To sum up, the Royal Marriages Act has virtually no impact on the marriages of those closest to the throne but remains a trap for those unaware that they need to comply with its provisions. It has been criticized almost since its inception, but reasons have always been found to defer reform. The only element of the original statute to have changed in the intervening years is the removal of the harsh penalties for those attending a marriage celebrated without royal consent.[129] The issue of reform will be considered further in the final section of this book, but we now need to turn our attention to other issues raised by the Catholic and civil weddings that have taken place in recent years. Does the law actually allow members of the royal family to marry in such ways?

chapter 4

The Royal Exemption from the General Law of Marriage

THE MOST uncertain and contentious aspect of the marriage law applying to members of the royal family relates to an exemption from the general law, rather than to specific legislation such as the Royal Marriages Act and the Act of Settlement. In England and Wales, marriage, which had for centuries been governed by the Church's canon law, was first subject to Parliamentary legislation in 1753. However, both the Clandestine Marriages Act of that year and each succeeding statute have specifically provided that such legislation does not apply to members of the royal family, and it is this exemption which lies at the heart of the current confusion.

From March 25th, 1754, the day the Clandestine Marriages Act came into force, the general population became subject to the new statutory regulations. But the Act stated that its provisions 'shall not extend to the Marriages of any of the Royal Family,'[1] and this meant that the marriages of members of the royal family continued to be governed by the canon law. The canon law itself subsequently, and somewhat confusingly, became known as 'common law' in this context to distinguish it from the new legislation,[2] a point that needs to be borne in mind when reading later claims about 'common-law marriage'. To understand the significance of the royal exemption, it is necessary to understand both what the canon law had required before that date, and precisely what changes were brought about by successive pieces of legislation.[3]

The Clandestine Marriages Act 1753

The Church's canon law had long laid down strict requirements relating to banns and licences, parental consent, and the time and place of marriage, although a marriage that failed to comply with these requirements was not necessarily void.[4] The only essential requirement before March 25th, 1754, was that the marriage should be conducted by an Anglican clergyman.

It has been widely but wrongly claimed that prior to that date it was possible to marry by a simple, private exchange of consent (e.g. 'I take you as my husband/wife'). This, however, is based on a misunderstanding of the law at the time. Although such an exchange was *binding* upon the parties (assuming, of course, that it could be proved to the satisfaction of the church courts, which was no easy matter), what it bound them to do was to solemnize their union before an Anglican clergyman. If either tried to renege upon the contract, the other had the right to insist on its performance—and the church courts would order the marriage to be celebrated in a church.

In some respects the Clandestine Marriages Act merely put the requirements of the canon law on a statutory basis without changing their effect. Many of the legislative requirements for a valid marriage were (then as now) directory rather than mandatory; that is to say, non-compliance with certain details would not affect the validity of the marriage. For example, although the Act specified that the marriage had to be conducted in the presence of two witnesses, who should then sign the register, the absence of such witnesses did not render the marriage void. In fact, even a complete failure to register the marriage did not affect its validity. The Act made no mention of the times of day when marriages could take place, and this detail therefore remained governed by canon law, which had allowed marriages only between the hours of eight in the morning and twelve noon. Again, though, marriages celebrated outside those hours were not void as a result.

On the other hand, the 1753 Act did contain novel—and crucial—annulling clauses. It stipulated that a marriage that was not preceded by the calling of banns or the obtaining of a licence was void, as was one that was not celebrated in a public church. A marriage by licence would also be void if either party was under the age of twenty-one and the consent of the relevant parent or guardian had not been obtained.

Set against this context, it is clear that the exemption of the royal family from the 1753 Act was intended to protect them against the effect of the annulling clauses introduced by the Act, rather than to signify that they were entitled to disregard the formalities relating to marriage altogether. Members of the royal family could still marry by banns or by licence, or simply by exchanging vows before an Anglican clergyman, just as they had before the Act. The exemption merely meant that the marriage remained valid even if they failed to observe the formalities demanded of the general population. Internationally important royal marriages, it seems, should not be undermined by possible future challenges over their validity.

There was perhaps one more reason for the exemption of members of the royal family from the requirements of the 1753 Act. Within the royal family, the consent of one's sovereign was by tradition more important than the consent of one's parent, but the wording of the Act specified that it was *parental* consent that was required for the marriages of certain minors to go ahead. Extending the Act to royalty would have risked creating a clash of authority between parents and the sovereign.[5]

But the exemption did not mean that members of the royal family were free to marry in any way they chose. At the very least the presence of an Anglican clergyman was required. So, when the Duke of Gloucester secretly married Maria Walpole in a private ceremony in her house in 1766, the marriage was valid according to the pre-1754 canon law, since it was conducted by her chaplain.[6] Similarly, it was a chaplain who conducted the marriage of the Duke of Cumberland to Anne Horton in 1771.[7] And, had it not been for the Royal Marriages Act's requiring of the King's consent, the Prince of Wales' marriage to Maria Fitzherbert in 1785 would have been perfectly valid, since the ceremony was conducted by one of the Prince's chaplains.[8] Of course, since Maria Fitzherbert was a Catholic, if their marriage *had* been valid then the Prince of Wales would have been barred from succeeding to the throne under the Act of Settlement—a perfect distillation of all three of the forces which govern royal marriage.

However, failure to observe the other requirements of the canon law was not without its consequences, even if the validity of the marriage itself was not affected. A clergyman who flouted the canonical requirements that a marriage be preceded by banns or licence and celebrated in church could be suspended from his post for three years.[9] Even after the 1753 Act, clergymen remained liable to punishment by the ecclesiastical courts for infringements of canon law not covered by the new legislation.[10] Although members of the royal family obviously had means of persuasion at their disposal not available to the general public, clergymen were fully aware that flouting the Church's rules had serious consequences.

And so the obvious solution for members of the royal family in the wake of the 1753 Act—and indeed for anybody who wished to marry with a degree of privacy rather than in a public church—was to marry by special licence. Special licences, granted by the Archbishop of Canterbury, removed the need for banns or licence or indeed any other formalities, and allowed a marriage to be conducted by an Anglican clergyman at any time or place. First introduced by the Ecclesiastical Licences Act of 1533, their availability had been confirmed both by the canons of 1604 and by the 1753 Act and proved invaluable: one nineteenth-century commentator noted that it was apparently 'invariable practice' for members of the royal family to marry by special licence.[11]

Even after 1754, then, the marriages of members of the royal family remained very different from those of the majority of their subjects in terms of the privacy with which they were celebrated. The Chapel Royal at St James's Palace was a favoured spot, being the location of the marriage of

George III's eldest sister Augusta in 1764[12] as well as that of his eldest son George in 1795.[13] Many royal marriages took place in other royal residences: when Princess Charlotte, the only legitimate child of the Prince Regent and second in line to the throne, married Prince Leopold of Saxe-Coburg-Saalfeld in May 1816, the wedding took place at her father's home, Carlton House, in the evening.[14] Similarly, after Charlotte's untimely death sparked a scramble to marry among her many uncles, the double wedding of the Dukes of Clarence and Kent (to Princess Adelaide of Saxe-Meiningen and Victoria Mary, the Dowager Princess of Saxe-Meiningen respectively) took place at their mother's home at Kew.[15]

The Marriage Act 1836

The annulling provisions of the Clandestine Marriages Act of 1753 were modified by a succession of Parliamentary acts in the 1820s, but in each successive piece of legislation an identical provision was expressly included, stipulating that it did not apply to members of the royal family.[16] The legislation that was passed in 1836, though, was different from its predecessors and marked a new era in the regulation of marriage. The acts passed in 1753 and in the 1820s had simply given the requirements of the Church the force of statute (and the penalty of invalidity should the parties fail to comply with certain provisions). The Marriage Act 1836, by contrast, introduced new modes of marriage for the first time, and it is here that the marriage practices of the general population began to diverge radically from those of royalty.

First, the 1836 Act made it possible to marry according to non-Anglican religious rites. While Jews and Quakers had been exempted from the 1753 Act, there had been no explicit statement as to whether their marriages would be recognised by law, leaving the courts to deal with disputed cases. Under the 1836 Act, however, their marriages were declared to be valid, as long as they observed the stipulated preliminaries.

Those who belonged to other non-Anglican denominations or faiths (including Catholics) could also legally marry according to their own rites for the first time, but were subject to greater regulation: not only were they required to observe certain preliminaries, but they were also required to marry in a place of worship that was licensed for marriage,[17] in the presence of a civil registrar.[18]

But more importantly for future royal marriages, the 1836 Act introduced the possibility of marrying in a purely civil ceremony, something that had previously only been available for a very brief period during Oliver Cromwell's Commonwealth.[19] Section 21 provided that those who objected to marriage in a registered place of worship might 'contract and solemnize Marriage at the Office and in the Presence of the Superintendent Registrar and some Registrar of the District, and in the Presence of Two Witnesses.' Such a ceremony had to be preceded by one of the new forms of civil preliminaries, modelled on the old options of banns and licences. The civil equivalent of banns involved notice of the marriage being given to the superintendent registrar of the district where each party had resided for the previous seven days, and that marriage notice being read out at weekly meetings of Poor Law Guardians on three successive occasions.[20] The more expensive licences, which cost £3 and reduced the waiting period to seven days, could be obtained from the superintendent registrar of the district.[21]

The 1836 Act, like its predecessors, still expressly stated that it did not extend to the marriages of members of the royal family,[22] but the effect of this section was crucially different from that of the equivalent sections in the legislation passed in 1753 and 1823. The earlier legislation had simply given force to the requirements of the canon law, and there was therefore nothing to prevent members of the royal family from marrying by banns or by licence if they so chose, since those formalities originated in the canon law of the Church of England. By contrast, when the 1836 Act stipulated that it did not extend to members of the royal family, this meant that they were not entitled to take advantage of any of the new modes of marriage introduced by that statute, including civil marriage. The privilege conferred by the exemptions in the 1753 and 1823 Acts became, after 1836, a restriction on how royalty could marry.

The possibility of members of the royal family marrying in a civil ceremony was not even canvassed in the Parliamentary debates. This was unsurprising, since it was not expected that this form of marriage would be popular, and it was scarcely thinkable that royalty would choose to marry in this way. Both assumptions were borne out by events. Throughout the nineteenth century, relatively few couples even amongst the general population chose to marry in a civil ceremony.[23] As noted above, the new forms of marriage introduced by the 1836 Act suffered from the stigma of association with the machinery of the Poor Law,[24] and many of the first batch of civil registrars to be appointed were officers of a Poor Law Union.[25] Royalty were hardly likely to jump at the chance of a civil marriage. Finally, the issue of which forms of marriage should be available to members of the royal family was perhaps, like today, rather too sensitive an issue for Parliament to confront. Too many of the royal dukes and even the sovereign, King William IV, had pasts that would not bear close examination.[26]

The new debate over 'common-law marriage'

The fact that members of the royal family did not have the right to marry in a civil ceremony under the 1836 Act was unquestioned, yet new developments in the courts were to raise the possibility of their taking advantage of a less formal mode of marriage. A quarter of a century earlier, in 1811, the ecclesiastical judge Sir William Scott had suggested in a landmark case called *Dalrymple v Dalrymple* that it had been possible to marry in England and Wales before the

Clandestine Marriages Act of 1753 by simply exchanging vows (e.g. 'I take you as my husband/wife'), without even the need for an Anglican clergyman to be present. If Sir William Scott were right, it would of course mean that members of the royal family could continue to marry by such simple means after the Act, too.

Sir William's judgment was, however, based on some very big assumptions. For a start, the case of *Dalrymple* involved events that had taken place in Scotland, which has its own very distinct legal system. Untrained in Scottish law, Sir William spoke frankly of his 'inferior qualifications' to decide the matter. His discussion of English law occupied less than a page, and the legal authorities he cited lent little support to his conclusion that it had been possible to marry by a simple exchange of vows before March 25th, 1754. The House of Lords had the opportunity to scotch Sir William Scott's mistaken assertion when the case of *R v Millis* came before them in the 1840s.[27] I will spare the reader a detailed account of the facts: in a nutshell, George Millis had married one woman in Ireland and another in England, but whether he was guilty of bigamy depended on the legal status of the Irish marriage, which had been celebrated before a Presbyterian minister.[28] And this in turn depended on whether it was possible to marry without an Anglican clergyman present—in essence, whether a simple exchange of vows would suffice.

It was understandable—if unfortunate—that the judges' understanding of the law that had applied ninety years earlier should be somewhat garbled. Three held that an exchange of vows created a valid marriage—and three held that it did not. Given this deadlock, the presumption in favour of innocence applied, and George Millis was acquitted. This result, while happy for George, was disastrous for the law. The case had to be taken as deciding that a mere exchange of vows did not create a valid marriage, but so superficially convincing were those who had argued that it did, and so far had Sir William Scott's claims in *Dalrymple* seeped into the legal consciousness, that scholarly opinion ranged itself on the losing side. *R v Millis* therefore has the unenviable distinction of being almost universally derided as wrongly decided.

But even those who took the view that *R v Millis* was wrongly decided concurred that it would nevertheless be binding on any subsequent court.[29] The essential point for our present purposes is that, after *Millis* was decided in 1844, it became axiomatic that it was not—and never had been—possible for a member of the royal family, or indeed anybody else, to marry in England and Wales simply by exchanging vows. It was understood that for royalty to enter into a valid marriage in this jurisdiction there needed to be an Anglican clergyman presiding. Still, the perception that *Millis* was wrong, and that a simple exchange of vows was sufficient, remained academic orthodoxy—and was to re-emerge in public debate 160 years later.[30]

From the dining room to the abbey

In the meantime, just as would be expected, there seems to have been not a single example of a member of the royal family marrying according to non-Anglican rites in England and Wales in the nineteenth century. While some of Queen Victoria's children married in relatively private ceremonies, all those that took place in England and Wales were conducted according to the rites of the Church of England. The marriage of Princess Alice to the future Grand Duke of Hesse, for example, took place at Osborne House on the Isle of Wight, the dining room having been 'turned into a temporary chapel' for the occasion.[31] Despite its unconventional location, no less a personage than the Archbishop of Canterbury himself conducted the marriage.

From the early twentieth century, as we have seen, royal marriages began to be celebrated with a greater degree of publicity. The *Morning Post* mused in 1934 that 'One of the King's happy thoughts in his most happy reign has taken shape in the recognition of the Abbey Church of Westminster as the correct theatre for the celebration of Royal marriages.[32] Not only the invited guests of the Abbey, but an enormous public will find keen enjoyment in a National function, an enjoyment formerly denied to them by the narrow circumstances of the Chapel Royal or by the distance of St George's Chapel, Windsor, from the Metropolis.' (The marriage alluded to was that of the Duke of Kent to Princess Marina of Greece,[33] which was in fact highly unusual in involving two sets of marriage rites. The Anglican ceremony in Westminster Abbey was followed by a Greek Orthodox one held in Buckingham Palace.[34] Given the terms of the 1836 Act, the Greek Orthodox ceremony alone would not of course have created a valid marriage.)

There arose, though, at least one occasion on which the possibility of a member of the royal family marrying according to non-Anglican rites was considered by the authorities. In January 1941 *The Times* announced the engagement of Lady Iris Mountbatten, a great-granddaughter of Queen Victoria, to Captain O'Malley.[35] Since the Captain was Catholic, it was intended that the marriage should take place at Brompton Oratory, and this was duly reported in the press.[36]

The question then arose as to whether it was actually possible for Lady Iris to marry in a Catholic ceremony. The Attorney-General Sir Donald Somervell, and Sir William Jowitt, the Solicitor-General, were asked as the Law Officers of the Crown to provide an opinion on the point. Concluding that Lady Iris, a great-granddaughter of Queen Victoria, was a member of the royal family, they noted that '[i]n consequence, the various Marriage Acts do not apply to her and it is necessary to consider the position at common law.'[37]

Having reviewed the decision in the case of *R v Millis* and noted how 'from the Reformation until the Marriage Act of 1836 Roman Catholics in fact went through a Church of England ceremony, clearly on the assumption that a marriage before a Roman Catholic priest would not be a valid marriage,'

Somervell and Jowitt correctly concluded that 'a marriage between Lady Iris Mountbatten and Captain O'Malley in a Roman Catholic church would not be a valid marriage.'[38]

The Roman Catholic authorities having indicated that they would accept a Church of England ceremony taking place, Lady Iris and her Captain married in the Anglican parish church of St Mary's, Balcombe, in Sussex. This was followed by a seven-minute ceremony at the Roman Catholic church of St Paul's, Haywards Heath—as a scribbled comment in the official file noted, 'they always set it down to the bare minimum where one of the parties is a heretic.'[39]

Lady Iris' marriage to the Captain might have been short-lived—they divorced in 1946—but it served to confirm that the only mode of marriage open to members of the royal family at this time was one conducted according to the rites of the Church of England. The discussions also confirmed the continuing importance of *Millis* and its application to the marriages of members of the royal family. One senior civil servant, Sir Rupert Howorth, noted wryly that the prediction of two scholars that the point it decided was unlikely to be of any practical importance in the future was 'an example of the frailty of human prophecy!'[40]

The Marriage Act 1949

Over the course of the nineteenth and early twentieth centuries there were repeated minor amendments to the Marriage Act 1836, and by the middle of the twentieth century it was deemed desirable to consolidate these disparate pieces of legislation into one statute. The subsequent Marriage Act 1949 was one of the first pieces of legislation to be passed under the Consolidation of Enactments (Procedure) Act 1949, which introduced a new procedure for the consideration of such consolidation measures.[41] The draft Marriage Bill was the very first to be considered by the Joint Committee of the Houses of Parliament, and it is clear from the preliminary discussions of that Committee that its members were mindful of the limitations within which they had to operate. The Marquess of Reading, chairing the Committee, noted that:

'We have to remember that the only alterations we can make in existing Acts and incorporate in the new Bill are corrections and minor improvements.... In other words, if we think that although a change may be desirable it is not within the definition of a correction or minor improvement, we cannot insert it.'[42]

The Consolidation of Enactments (Procedure) Act 1949 was very clear on what constituted a 'correction or minor improvement', i.e.:

'amendments of which the effect is confined to resolving ambiguities, removing doubts, bringing obsolete provisions into conformity with modern practice, or removing unnecessary provisions or anomalies which are not of substantial importance, and amendments designed to facilitate improvement in the form or manner in which the law is stated.'[43]

It also specified that corrections and minor improvements could not be approved by either the Joint Committee or the Lord Chancellor if they effected changes 'in the existing law of such importance that they ought... to be separately enacted by Parliament.'[44]

Such dry details are crucial to a proper understanding of the clause dealing with marriages of members of the royal family. It was clear that the Act was not intended to change the law in any material respect, and it is against that background that we should read the provision in the Marriage Act 1949 that '[n]othing in this Act is intended to affect any law or custom relating to marriages of the Royal Family.'[45] Since before 1949 there had unarguably been no law or custom allowing them to marry otherwise than according to the rites of the Church of England, the obvious meaning of this provision was that other forms of marriages did not become an option as a result of the 1949 Act.

Given that the Joint Committee discussed some very minor amendments (for example the substitution of 'calendar month' for 'month' to bring Anglican marriages into conformity with non-Anglican ones[46]) it is inconceivable that a change in the modes of marriage available to members of the royal family would not have been seen as a matter worthy of the most intense discussion. Yet there is not the slightest reference to the subject in the report of the Committee. It is equally unlikely that the drafters of the new Bill would have chosen to convey so important a change in the law in such an elliptical fashion as a minor and unremarked change of wording. In any case, there is a presumption that legislation enacted to consolidate a law was not intended to change that law. This is one of the basic principles of statutory interpretation that will be applied by any court considering a disputed provision.[47]

It is true that the words used in the 1949 Act are not exactly the same as those in the 1836 Act, or indeed in any of the other pieces of marriage legislation consolidated in 1949, and it is important to address this discrepancy. For one thing, there is a reference to 'custom' in the 1949 Act that does not appear in the earlier versions. In addition, the 1949 Act provides that it does not 'affect' the existing laws and customs applicable to royal marriages, while earlier Acts simply provided that they did not 'extend' to members of the royal family. But there were good reasons for both of these minor changes.

Files in the National Archives record the anxious discussions behind the scenes about the royal family's idiosyncratic method of registering marriages. The Royal Marriage Register was in the keeping of the sovereign: when a member of the royal family married, the register was delivered to the church for the ceremony, and then returned.[48] It appears to have been agreed as far back as 1843 that the marriages of members of the royal family would be exempt from the usual registration requirement, but at least one official thought that greater certainty would be desirable 'if this could be done without creating the impression that the Royal Family have been law breakers for the last hundred years.'[49] As so often, however, the view prevailed that even if reform might in theory be desirable this was not the right time to effect it, and that '[o]n the whole it would seem best to leave things as they are.' The actual papers in the National Archives are so dog-eared and torn, sometimes with a crucial word lost to posterity, that it is not always easy to work out what is being discussed, but it seems to have been thought that the reference to 'custom' in the draft Bill would be a satisfactory way of addressing the issue.

Similarly, the reason for the change in the phrasing of the royal exemption—from 'extend to' to 'affect'—is a very simple one. The Marriage Acts passed in 1753, 1823 and 1836 had dealt only with the formalities necessary for a valid marriage. By contrast, the Marriage Act 1949, in codifying most of the existing statutes on marriage, also covered the legal age of marriage,[50] the requirement of parental consent[51] and the prohibited degrees of marriage.[52] If the 1949 Act had stipulated that it did not 'extend to' members of the royal family, this would have meant that they could therefore ignore the provisions on minimum age, prohibited degrees and so on. In this light, to have persisted with the same words as before would have caused a radical change in the law, a move totally at odds with the explicit aims of the Act's drafters. Indeed, in early drafts it was still being stated that Parts II and III of the Act, dealing with the formal procedures for marriages, would not 'extend' to the marriages of members of the royal family, and only when the exemption clause was made applicable to all of the provisions in the Act was the wording changed to 'affect'.[53]

The wording of the Marriage Act 1949, then, was skilfully crafted to convey that no change in the law applicable to members of the royal family was intended. So, if members of the royal family *had* been bound by the general law prior to 1949—for example by the rules setting a minimum age of marriage and laying out the prohibited degrees—they would *continue* to be bound; if, however, a particular law had *not* extended to members of the royal family before 1949—for example that on marriages according to non-Anglican rites—it would still *not* do so after that time.

Royal remarriages

This was certainly the interpretation that prevailed in the years that followed. At the time of Princess Margaret's mooted marriage to Peter Townsend, for example, there was extensive discussion of the form that any such marriage might take. Given that the Church of England had set its face against the remarriage of divorcees in church, an Anglican wedding was out of the question. The Church even had legislative sanction for such refusal: when judicial divorce was introduced in 1857, the Act provided that no clergyman of the Church of England would be obliged to solemnize the marriage of any divorced person whose spouse was still living.

But the exclusion of members of the royal family from the legislation governing marriage meant that, according to a note on royal marriages from the Lord Chancellor's Office which had apparently been 'put together from the best sources available,' they 'cannot legally be married in a Registry Office in England.' The upshot was that it might be impossible for a member of the royal family to marry a divorcee in England at all, 'since a Registrar could not and the Church would not perform the ceremony.'[54]

Such was the interpretation advanced by the then Lord Chancellor, Lord Kilmuir, when advising the Cabinet in 1955:

'marriages of members of the royal family are still not in the same position as marriages of other persons, for such marriages have always been expressly excluded from the Statutes about marriage in England and Wales, and marriage abroad, and are therefore governed by the common law. This means that, in England and Wales, such a marriage can be validly celebrated only by a clergyman of the Church of England. A civil marriage before the Registrar and marriage according to the rights of any Church other than the Church of England are not possible.'[55]

And, tellingly, when Princess Margaret announced that she was not going to marry Peter Townsend, she noted that contracting a civil marriage would have depended on 'my renouncing my rights of succession.'[56] In short, it was understood that civil marriage—at least in England or Wales—was not a possibility while Margaret remained a member of the royal family.

The question of precisely where such a marriage *could* take place arose once again when the divorced Earl of Harewood wished to marry Patricia Tuckwell. As the Earl recorded in his autobiography, since a civil marriage was not an option for members of the royal family, 'banns and a church wedding were therefore necessary for us in England (but for divorcees unavailable), and things were not much easier in Scotland and Wales.'[57] As the couple considered their options, every way seemed barred. They 'discovered that notice of some kind was needed in France, Germany and Scandinavia [and] that only Roman Catholics seemed to be legally wed in Italy and Spain.' Even the Lebanon was contemplated, but here 'only Muslim or Catholic marriages existed.' Finally, they concluded, '[o]ur best bet seemed to be America.'[58]

Even then their troubles were not at an end. Staying with a friend in New York, it was clear that marriage in the state was not an option, since its law forbade remarriage so soon after a divorce. So, Harewood noted, 'we needed an uninquisitive registry office somewhere close to New York… someone with a knowledge of American law to tell us what was required before the ceremony could take place, and a discreet Justice of the Peace to make it all legal.'[59] They eventually registered their intentions at New Canaan in Connecticut—having undergone the test for syphilis that state law required—and married in a garden made available to them by a client of their lawyer.[60]

Not long after, the Earl of Harewood's brother Gerald Lascelles married the former actress Elizabeth Colvin after they had lived together for twenty years, having only obtained a divorce from his first wife Angela Dowding earlier that year.[61] This marriage took place in Vienna in 1978, and for the same reasons: civil marriage in England and Wales was not possible for Gerald as a member of the royal family, while his divorce precluded marriage in church.

Two of the Earl of Harewood's sons from his first marriage also subsequently divorced and remarried. The eldest, Viscount Lascelles, married his second wife in Adelaide in South Australia.[62] The Earl's second son, James, had an even more chequered matrimonial career. Married to an American student in 1973, the young couple shared James' Norfolk manor house with an assortment of like-minded residents, living what the papers described as 'a hippie-style existence'. After divorcing in 1985, James travelled the world and met the woman who became his second wife, a Native American known as 'Shadow', and married her in Albuquerque, New Mexico. After *that* marriage ended in divorce in 1997, he returned to London and met Joy Elias-Rilwan, a Nigerian actress. In January 1999 the *Mail on Sunday* reported the 'secret wedding of a Roedean runaway and the hippy of the House of Windsor', noting that the marriage had taken place 'on a sunswept beach' in the West Indies. Again, the attentive reader will have noted something that all these weddings had in common (apart from the predilection of this particular branch of the royal family for actresses and models): while those marrying for the first time tied the knot in England and Wales, every single second or subsequent marriage took place overseas.

Indeed, before 2005, not only had no descendant of Edward VII ever married in a civil ceremony in England and Wales,[63] but neither had any one of them married in this jurisdiction other than according to Anglican rites. When the marriage of Prince Michael of Kent to the Catholic Baroness Marie-Christine von Reibnitz was mooted in the 1970s, the couple wished to marry in a Catholic church: tellingly, it was intended that the wedding should take place in Vienna rather than in England and Wales, where the couple were then resident. In the event, after the Pope's refusal to issue a dispensation for the marriage to go ahead, they married in a civil ceremony in Vienna's town hall instead.[64]

Similarly, when in 1992 Princess Anne married Timothy Lawrence after her divorce from Mark Phillips, the wedding took place at Crathie Kirk, Balmoral, the Church of Scotland having more liberal views on the remarriage of divorcees than the Church of England. One journalist noted astutely at the time that Anne's brother Charles might face problems were he to divorce and wish to remarry:

'[a] defect or omission in the 1949 legislation on civil marriage means he could not marry in a register office in England without an amending act of parliament.'[65]

In the event, no such legislation was passed before Prince Charles' marriage in Windsor Guildhall in 2005. The story of how government officials claimed that the law *did* allow members of the royal family to marry in a civil ceremony will be told in the next chapter.

chapter 5

Royal Restrictions in an
Era of Human Rights

SO, MEMBERS of the royal family are subject to a number of restrictions when entering into a marriage. Descendants of George II have required the consent of the monarch in order to marry; those who marry a Catholic have forfeited any right to the throne; and members of the royal family have not been able to marry in ceremonies other than those of the Church of England. But can those restrictions survive in an era of human rights?

I should warn readers that the legal arguments are going to get more complex in this chapter, and that there will be fewer stories about the marriages of individual royal personages. But the full uncertainty of the law as it now stands cannot be appreciated without a detailed explanation of the events of 2005 and the arguments that were then advanced about how the Human Rights Act might change the law applicable to royal marriages. One possibility is that none of the restrictions outlined in the previous three chapters would survive a challenge under human rights law. But another is that they remain in full force and that future royal marriages may be vulnerable to challenge because of erroneous assumptions about what limitations actually survive. The fact that two such dramatically different interpretations are possible is a measure of the authorities' failure to clarify the situation when the opportunity presented itself.

Let us turn first to the innocent-sounding provisions that might lead to such different conclusions. Article 12 of the European Convention on Human Rights provides that 'men and women of marriageable age have the right to marry and found a family' but adds, crucially, 'according to the national laws governing the exercise of this right.' A state has the right to set minimum requirements relating to age and capacity to marry, to prohibit marriages between those closely related by blood, and to prevent individuals from being married to more than one person at the same time. It also has the right to prescribe the formalities that must be observed, and individuals will be expected to observe them. The law might, however, violate Article 12 if it imposed restrictions on marriage 'in such a way or to such an extent that the very essence of the right is impaired.'[1] In other words, a state cannot enact a marriage law that is so restrictive as to negate any genuine right to marry. Thus, for example, the European Court of Human Rights has in the past held that denying serving prisoners the right to marry was a breach of Article 12,[2] as were blanket restrictions placed on all those subject to immigration control, regardless of whether their intended marriage was genuine.[3]

The United Kingdom was one of the original signatories to the European Convention, ratifying it as long ago as 1951, but it is since the incorporation of the Convention into UK law by the Human Rights Act in 1998 that its effect has really been felt. Judges and other decision-makers are today required to interpret the law in a way that is compatible with the Convention.[4] Of course, the extent to which words in a statute can be 'interpreted' to bear a particular meaning is not infinite. If the legislation in question is simply incompatible with the Convention, then it is up to a court to issue a declaration of incompatibility,[5] and for Parliament, in due course, to legislate to amend the offending provision.

In the last ten years the English courts have held that a number of aspects of the law of marriage are in breach of the European Convention. In 2003, for example, the House of Lords held that the fact that the law did not permit a transsexual to marry in his or her reassigned sex was a violation of Article 12.[6] In 2008 it was suggested that requiring those subject to immigration control to pay a fee of £295 each when giving notice of their intention to marry was objectionable, since 'a fee fixed at a level which a needy applicant cannot afford may impair the essence of the right to marry.'[7] And in December 2010 the Court of Appeal held that a rule preventing those under the age of 21 from acting as a sponsor to a spouse from other country violated the rights of those concerned.[8]

These cases illustrate the increasing importance attached to human rights issues in the courts, but they also illustrate two crucial points about the operation of the Human Rights Act. The first is that the court may decide that the rights of a particular couple have been violated, without going so far as to decide that the impugned rule or scheme should be struck down in its entirety. This was the case in, for example, the case of the two young couples who challenged the rules on the entry of foreign spouses: the Court of Appeal was very clear that it was deciding these two cases on their own facts, 'leaving it to the Home Secretary... to decide how far their ripples spread.'[9] The second point is that even a finding that the law does not comply with the Convention does not mean that it is thereby instantly reformed, as though a magic wand had been waved. Thus, for example, the rights of transsexuals were dealt with by primary legislation, after both the European Court of Rights and the House of Lords had declared UK law to be in breach of the Convention.[10] Even after the Lords' decision, almost two years were to elapse before transsexuals could apply to obtain formal recognition of their reassigned sex, a necessary step before marrying, and any hoping to marry in the meantime had simply to wait.[11] The higher fee for those marrying while subject to immigration control continued to apply until it was formally suspended, almost a year after the House of Lords had decided that it was contrary to Article 12, and even then it took the instigation of judicial review proceedings to force the government to act.[12]

An appreciation of such subtleties is essential as we come to consider how the restrictions on marriages of members of the royal family should be dealt with in an era of human rights. The question has acquired new urgency because, in the wake of the marriage of Prince Charles and Camilla Parker Bowles in 2005, it now seems to be assumed that members of the royal family can marry in any of the ways laid down by statute. As we shall see, the Human Rights Act was one of the reasons given for this assumption in 2005. But there was never any satisfying explanation of *why* the Human Rights Act would allow this particular couple to marry in a civil ceremony. Nor was there any discussion of how the Marriage Act 1949 as a whole would apply to members of the royal family. And if the restrictions on the available forms of marriage ceremony can apparently vanish with the mere mention of human rights, where does that leave the far more discriminatory provisions of the Act of Settlement or the additional preliminaries imposed by the Royal Marriages Act?

To answer these questions, I will look first at the doubts over the availability of civil marriage that dogged the announcement of Prince Charles' engagement to Camilla. I will then go on to consider whether the couple's right to marry would have been infringed had such a marriage not been available to them, and whether the rights of members of the royal family more generally are violated by a restriction on the forms of marriage available. But, as we have just seen, the fact that a law is in breach of the Convention does not mean that it no longer exists. So it is necessary to consider whether the Marriage Act 1949 could indeed be interpreted in the way that the authorities contended in 2005 or whether, as many thought, legislation would be necessary in order to allow members of the royal family to marry other than according to the rites of the Church of England.

The first royal civil marriage in England and Wales

When the separation of Charles and Diana was announced in 1992, there were initially said to be no plans for a divorce, and that in the event of Charles becoming King, Diana would still automatically become Queen.[13] But after the emotive interview on the BBC television programme *Panorama* in 1995, the Queen wrote to both Charles and Diana to advise them that an early divorce would be desirable, and by August of 1996 the heir to the throne had become a divorcee.

Around this time there was discussion at the highest levels of government about the potential remarriage of the Prince of Wales, although it was stressed that this was a purely hypothetical issue. An undated Cabinet Office briefing noted that

> '[m]embers of the Royal Family are excepted from the provisions of the Marriage Act 1949, and their marriages in England and Wales must therefore be performed by Anglican clergy under either a Special or a Common Licence.'[14]

As speculation grew about a possible marriage between Prince Charles and Camilla Parker Bowles, journalists commented on the form that such a marriage might take. In 2001, an article in *The Spectator* suggested that the Prince of Wales could marry in a civil ceremony; a week later, however, it published a letter from the pre-eminent family lawyer Dr Stephen Cretney, Emeritus Fellow of All Souls' College, Oxford, pointing out that 'the legislation under which civil marriages take place in this country does not apply to members of the royal family.' The *Daily Mail* made the same point:

> '[t]alk of Charles and Camilla marrying in a civil ceremony... is wrong on technical grounds. Under the 1836 Act which allowed civil marriages, royals are banned from such ceremonies.'[15]

Given this widespread awareness of the legal background, it was therefore with considerable bemusement that legal experts and other commentators read the announcement on February 10th, 2005, that the Prince of Wales and Camilla

Parker Bowles planned to marry in a civil wedding in Windsor Castle. Four days later, the BBC broadcast an edition of *Panorama* in which a number of legal experts cast doubt on the possibility of members of the royal family marrying in a civil ceremony and pointed out the problems of securing approval for civil weddings to take place in Windsor Castle.[16] While some regarded these experts as little more than inconsiderate troublemakers,[17] it is clear that they were motivated by a sense of public responsibility. When, one might ask, should they have disclosed their concerns? Would it have been any less embarrassing for Clarence House to find out only later that it was not possible for the marriage to take place in Windsor Castle? Imagine having to write to the illustrious guests to inform them that the venue had been changed on account of a perfectly foreseeable legal obstacle.

The possibility of a civil marriage in Windsor Castle

Even setting aside the special rules governing royal marriages, the suggestion that the wedding was to take place in Windsor Castle suggested that the Prince and his bride-to-be had been badly advised. Of course, given the royal family's exemption from the statutory rules on marriage, it would certainly be possible for a royal wedding to take place in Windsor Castle—or indeed anywhere else—as long as it was celebrated by an Anglican clergyman. As I have shown, prior to the Clandestine Marriages Act of 1753 this had been the only formal element necessary for an exchange of vows to constitute a valid marriage, and royal weddings had often taken place in private residences. Civil weddings, though, are more tightly regulated, a fact which escaped the attention of Prince Charles' legal advisors.

It is perhaps understandable, in view of headlines of couples exchanging vows on the London Eye, in football stadia, or even in supermarkets, that it should be assumed that it is possible to marry anywhere these days. But this is far from being the case. Under English law a civil marriage can only take place in a register office or in premises approved for civil marriage by a local authority. It is not possible to obtain 'one-off' approval for a specific marriage: licences run for a minimum of three years, and the venue must be available to all comers during that period.[18] As Dr Stephen Cretney commented with characteristic understatement, '[t]he improbability of the Royal Family wishing to have such provisions applying to Windsor Castle immediately suggested... that the Clarence House announcement on 10 February 2005 about the plans for the Prince's intended marriage had not taken into account all the relevant legal considerations.'[19] The venue for the proposed marriage was hastily changed to Windsor Guildhall, which *was* licensed for civil marriage. As one journalist wrote, on noting the switch, 'royal aides seem either to have overlooked the matter or been badly advised.'[20] The latter appears to have been the case: the *Daily Telegraph* later reported one courtier as saying that there had been 'preliminary discussions regarding the rules of getting a wedding licence and we were aware of the rules, but we had been given some initial advice that we could have it there anyway.... The advice only came through afterwards that we should use the Guildhall.'[21] One can understand royal aides wishing to be cautious in their enquiries before the wedding had been announced,[22] but there was nothing to prevent them consulting any of the standard textbooks on family law.

The possibility of a civil marriage in England and Wales

But the implicit assumption that members of the royal family *could* now marry in a civil ceremony continued to be debated. A few days later, the Lord Chancellor, Charles Falconer, granted an interview to the *Mail on Sunday*, loftily stating that he was 'certain' that this interpretation of the 1949 Act was the right one and blustering that those who disputed it 'may not have had time to think it through fully.' The headline under which these assertions appeared, however, suggested that the *Mail* was unconvinced: 'Charles Wedding Illegal Warn Experts.'[23] The key expert in question, Dr Stephen Cretney of All Souls', Oxford, was trenchant:

> 'They did not check the law properly. If they had, they would have seen in three seconds that what is proposed is legal nonsense. This has all the hallmarks of a typical Tony Blair approach whereby Prince Charles was told by the Government, 'You think marrying Camilla is going to be difficult, but it's all very easy and we can help you do it.' The law is not that simple. I still believe they cannot marry in a civil ceremony. Any prudent person would enact legislation making it absolutely clear that it is legal for a member of the Royal Family to contract a valid civil marriage.'

Some observers suggested that it was not necessary for members of the royal family to marry according to any form at all. The legal journalist Joshua Rozenberg, for example, suggested that if members of the royal family were not required to comply with the usual formalities of marriage 'they could conduct a "common law marriage" by simply living together.'[24] A 'leading constitutional lawyer' claimed in *The Times* that a declaration of intent would be sufficient: 'You have to declare it—you have to say "We are setting up as man and wife", but it's a failsafe.'[25] Though motivated no doubt by a desire to be helpful, both were simply wrong in those assertions: as explained in chapter four, the canon law of marriage (which continues to apply to members of the royal family if they are exempted from compliance with the statutory provisions) required, at the very least, vows to be exchanged before an Anglican clergyman.

The diversity of views being advanced doubtless served only to confuse issues still further. Lord Falconer had some justification in professing himself to be 'amazed… at the sudden rash of experts on royal marriages.'[26] But those whom he named—Valentine le Grice, Sir Nicholas Lyell, and Dr

Stephen Cretney—were hardly 'sudden' experts. Valentine le Grice was a highly respected QC who had practised in the field of family law since 1979; Lyell, Attorney-General for five years under John Major, would have been privy to the discussions over the separation and divorce of Charles and Diana; while Dr Stephen Cretney, a former Law Commissioner, had not only written the definitive history of the making of twentieth-century family law but had also written specifically about royal marriage in the country's leading law journal.[27] If Lord Falconer was unaware of Dr Cretney's credentials for commenting on the law in this area, one has to wonder how far his own researches had extended.

The Lord Chancellor's statement

On February 24th, 2005, Lord Falconer attempted to put an end to the discussion by issuing a Written Ministerial Statement.[28] It is worth quoting in full for a number of reasons. The first is to demonstrate its relative brevity: at a mere 417 words it is hardly a detailed account of the law, and much of the detail is mere persiflage. The second is to show just how much Lord Falconer's claims as to the possibility of a royal civil marriage rested on assertion rather than fact: his statement is littered with phrases such as 'in our view', 'we consider' and 'we are clear'. The third, of course, is for the reader to be satisfied that the criticisms that follow are justified and that no twist of the reasoning has been overlooked. It should be borne in mind here that the precise nature of the advice contained in the official files remains a matter of conjecture: Lord Falconer's Written Ministerial Statement was a matter of public record, but successive Freedom of Information requests to open the files in full have been turned down. It might be that they do contain, as subsequent refusals to open the files have implied, personal details which are too sensitive to be released (a point I address further below); or it might be that they simply contain nothing more convincing than the arguments already in the public domain, a revelation which would be embarrassing to those involved. At the time of the controversy, no other pertinent points were raised by those speaking for the government, and it would be hard to imagine what additional arguments could be made. In the face of refusals to subject the files to scrutiny, we must deal with what was deemed suitable for public consumption. This is what Lord Falconer said:

'The Government is satisfied that it is lawful for the Prince of Wales and Mrs Parker Bowles, like anyone else, to marry by a civil ceremony in accordance with Part III of the Marriage Act 1949.

'Civil marriages were introduced in England by the Marriage Act 1836. Section 45 said that the Act: "...shall not extend to the marriage of any of the Royal Family."

'But the provisions on civil marriage in the 1836 Act were repealed by the Marriage Act 1949. All remaining parts of the 1836 Act, including section 45, were repealed by the Registration Service Act 1953. No part of the 1836 Act therefore remains on the statute book.

'The Marriage Act 1949 re-enacted and re-stated the law on marriage in England and Wales. The Act covered both marriage by Church of England rite, and civil marriage. It did not repeat the language of section 45 of the 1836 Act. Instead, section 79(5) of the 1949 Act says that: "Nothing in this Act shall affect any law or custom relating to the marriage of members of the Royal Family."

'The change of wording is important, and the significance is not undermined by the fact that the 1949 Act is described as a consolidation Act. The interpretation of any Act of Parliament, even when it consolidates previous legislation, must be based on the words used in the Act itself, not different words used in the previous legislation.

'In our view, section 79(5) of the 1949 Act preserves ancient procedures applying to royal marriages, for example the availability of customary forms of marriage and registration. It also preserves the effect of the Royal Marriages Act 1772, which requires the Sovereign's consent for certain marriages. But it does not have the effect of excluding royal marriages from the scope of Part III, which provides for civil ceremonies. As the heading to section 79 indicates ('Repeals and savings') it is a saving, not an exclusion.

'We are aware that different views have been taken in the past; but we consider that these were over-cautious, and we are clear that the interpretation I have set out in this statement is correct. We also note that the Human Rights Act has since 2000 required legislation to be interpreted wherever possible in a way that is compatible with the right to marry (article 12) and with the right to enjoy that right without discrimination (article 14). This, in our view, puts the modern meaning of the 1949 Act beyond doubt.'

Readers might already have spotted flaws in the reasoning employed here, but it is worth spelling out those flaws, even if to do so requires considerably more words than the original statement.

First, Lord Falconer implied that the objections to members of the royal family marrying in a civil ceremony are based on the 1836 Act, and therefore spent some time emphasizing that that particular piece of legislation had been repealed. Hence his reference to the Registration Service Act 1953, a tactic which, in the words of Pooh-Bah, the Lord High Everything Else in the *Mikado*, is 'merely corroborative detail, intended to give artistic verisimilitude to a bald and unconvincing narrative.'[29] The argument that members of the royal family cannot marry in a civil ceremony does *not* rest on the terms of the now-repealed 1836 Act, but on the terms of the 1949 Act.

Lord Falconer was of course right to say that the interpretation of an Act of Parliament must be based on the words that are actually used. But, as touched on previously, there is a basic presumption in English law that an Act intended to consolidate the existing law does not cause any change to that law. As a result, the onus is on those arguing for a change in interpretation to show that this was the intent of Parliament at the time. While Lord Falconer asserted that the change in wording in the 1949 Act was 'significant', it is far from clear how the phrase '[n]othing in this Act shall affect any law or custom relating to the marriage of members of the Royal Family' can be regarded as conferring a right to marry in a civil ceremony where no such right existed before. As we have seen, there were good reasons for the subtle change in wording between the 1836 Act and the 1949 Act that had nothing to do with the availability of civil marriage.

Lord Falconer went on to suggest that the 'laws and customs' being preserved by the 1949 Act were 'ancient procedures' such as 'the availability of customary forms of marriage and registration' and the Royal Marriages Act 1772. The reference to 'customary forms of marriage' suggests that he shared the common misconception that it was possible to marry in an informal ceremony prior to 1754, since this otherwise seems an odd way of referring to Anglican marriages, even those celebrated without due observance of all the formal requirements. Indeed, if this were the case it would explain why Lord Falconer seemed so unconcerned about the interpretation of the 1949 Act: if he believed that it was possible to marry by a simple exchange of consent prior to 1754, and that this right had been preserved for members of the royal family ever since, then he would also have believed that the vows exchanged in a civil ceremony would be sufficient to create a marriage.

To some extent his misunderstanding is excusable. It is only in recent years that the mistaken view has grown up that informal or 'customary' ceremonies were common before 1754.[30] This would explain why Lord Falconer took a different view of the law from his predecessors, whom he dismissed as 'over-cautious'. I have personally, however, spent a great deal of time untangling the series of misunderstandings on which ideas about informal ceremonies are based, and have written about this extensively elsewhere.[31] Suffice it to be reiterated here that the possibility of marrying according to a bare exchange of vows was not one available to members of the royal family, or indeed anyone else, before or after 1754.

There is also a fundamental contradiction in the way that Lord Falconer presented his argument. The implication of his words was that, firstly, the 1949 Act was intended to preserve the effect of the Royal Marriages Act, rather than leaving royal marriages to be dealt with by the provisions relating to parental consent in Part I of the 1949 Act; secondly, that royal marriages would not be vulnerable to challenge under Part II of the 1949 Act for non-compliance with the formalities required for an Anglican marriage; and, thirdly, that the registration of royal marriages would continue as before, rather than members of the royal family being required to comply with Part IV of the 1949 Act. In short, according to Lord Falconer the law relating to members of the royal family would be unaffected by Parts I, II and IV of the 1949 Act—but not by Part III, which provided for civil ceremonies.

Had those responsible for drafting the 1949 Act wished to allow members of the royal family to marry in a civil ceremony, it would have been an easy matter to draft it accordingly. Early drafts did not, after all, exempt members of the royal family from the provisions relating to registration. It would have been a simple matter to preserve the privileges of the royal family in relation to Anglican marriages while not barring them from other forms of marriage, by stating that 'nothing in Parts I, II and IV of this Act shall affect any law or custom relating to the marriage of members of the Royal Family.' As Joshua Rozenberg pointed out, 'there was nothing to stop the 1949 Act authorising [non-Anglican] marriages for the first time.'[32] But it did not do so.

The final argument advanced by Lord Falconer about the

drafting of the 1949 Act was the significance of the fact that the section exempting members of the royal family was in a section headed 'Repeals and savings': 'it is a saving, not an exclusion,' he asserted. Again, anybody unfamiliar with the subtleties of statutory interpretation might well have believed that this supported Lord Falconer's argument. Yet the standard guide to statutory interpretation clearly sets out that a 'saving' 'is taken not to be intended to confer any right which did not exist already.'[33] In other words, it would run contrary to the standard rules of statutory interpretation for a saving to confer a new right, such as the right to marry in a form not previously available. Relying on a heading would in any case seem a very slender basis on which to base so significant a change in the law.

In short, there was nothing in the 1949 Act to suggest that members of the royal family had the right to marry in a civil ceremony—or according to rites other than those of the Church of England—when they had not enjoyed those rights before, and nothing in Lord Falconer's statement to give any grounds for adopting a different interpretation. Whether this restriction breaches the right to marry laid down by the European Convention on Human Rights is a separate question to which we shall return—the impact of the Human Rights Act requires more discussion than the two sentences in Lord Falconer's statement—but the difficulty of interpreting the plain words of the statute to bear a different meaning is also crucial to the question of how the law can be brought into line with the Convention.

Yet despite the obvious deficiencies of Lord Falconer's statement to anyone familiar with the law, it was sufficiently cleverly crafted to satisfy many media commentators[34]—although one presumes that Rod Liddle, writing in *The Times*, was being sarcastic when he referred to its 'fine detail.'[35] Most now turned their attention to the irony of how the Prince's wedding seemed to have been saved by a piece of legislation—the Human Rights Act—of which he had been openly critical. Headlines such as 'Charles relies on rights law he despised to validate marriage' and 'Human Rights to the rescue of wedding' abounded.[36] Journalists in the *Guardian* wrote admiringly of how Lord Falconer had 'waited until the end of his statement to pull the Human Rights Act from the legal canon as a final weapon.'[37] The *Daily Mail* was more acerbic in pointing out that 'the Government is in such a panic over claims that the wedding may not be legal that the Lord Chancellor turns cartwheels to insist it is perfectly all right under a Human Rights Act that Charles himself once described as a threat to "a sane, civilised and ordered existence."'[38]

Legal experts, though, were unimpressed and unconvinced. The former Attorney-General Sir Nicholas Lyell described Lord Falconer's interpretation as 'tenuous', joining the calls for the legal position to be clarified by a short and simple piece of legislation. Dr Stephen Cretney, in a carefully worded statement, commented that 'on the material available to me, I cannot accept that the matter is free from doubt. I would have thought that there would be a strong argument for putting the law beyond doubt by means of a short Act of Parliament.'[39] As David Pannick QC dryly noted, 'If they can pass legislation to tackle suspect terrorists in four days, then there is no reason to think they can't pass legislation on the validity of the marriage of the heir to the throne.'[40]

The Conservatives helpfully indicated that the government would have their support should it prove necessary to pass legislation confirming that members of the royal family could marry in a civil ceremony. The Shadow Attorney-General, Dominic Grieve, noted that a bill would 'make quite a lot of sense,' adding wisely that 'whether they can rely on the Human Rights Act to confirm that a civil ceremony would be valid can only be tested in the courts. And one does not want to get to that position.'[41] According to the *Mail on Sunday*, officials were 'told to prepare to rush through an emergency law if necessary', the unnamed source adding that 'We hope to avoid it because we don't want the Government to be blamed.'[42] Nor were those who stated that there was no need for legislation any more reassuring, the *Daily Telegraph* reporting that:

> '[b]oth Lord Falconer's senior officials and Downing Street told *The Telegraph* that they could see 'no need' for a simple two-clause Bill to 'clear up' the confusion, although they admitted that, constitutionally, they were in 'unknown territory' and that no one could pronounce with any certainty on the likely outcome of any legal challenge to the forthcoming wedding, were one to be launched.'[43]

A challenge to the wedding going ahead?

And the likelihood of there being such a challenge remained a very real one. The day after Lord Falconer had issued his statement, the *Guardian* published an interview with one Father Paul Williamson, who had already filed written objections to the wedding and had declared his intention to object in person should his points be ignored.[44] It also published a helpful guide to any others wishing to file an objection, setting out the forms that would need to be completed, the procedure that would be followed once the objection had been received, and the address from which the forms should be requested.[45]

Barely a week later, it was reported that the Registrar-General for England and Wales, Len Cook, was 'conducting a formal investigation into claims that the civil ceremony is in breach of the law.'[46] Eleven objections were received and referred by the Superintendent Registrars for Chippenham and Cirencester before the deadline on March 4th.

The Registrar-General dismisses the challenge

Given the short timespan allowed for objections, it is perhaps unsurprising that few objections were received. One might also wonder whether those making such objections had the necessary legal training to advance the arguments against the possibility of a civil wedding as cogently as they might have done: examining the archives and relevant legal precedents takes considerably more than a few days, as I am acutely aware.

The objections were clearly not so detailed as to require lengthy investigation, for by March 8th, only four days after the deadline, the Registrar-General felt able to issue a statement declaring that the caveats that had been lodged 'ought not to obstruct' the issue of a certificate permitting the marriage.[47] Again, it is worth quoting his statement in full:

'The principal grounds of objection are that the law does not allow The Prince of Wales to marry in a civil ceremony because: members of the Royal Family are a special category; special rules apply to this category; and, section 79(5) of the Marriage Act 1949 states that "Nothing in this Act shall affect any law or custom relating to the marriage of members of the Royal Family" and the provisions of the 1949 Act governing civil marriages do not therefore apply to marriages of members of the Royal Family. I have examined into this matter and I am satisfied that it ought not to obstruct the issue of a certificate because:

'the natural reading of section 79(5) is that it preserves, for example, the Royal Marriages Act 1772, and the custom of the Royal Family to maintain a Royal Marriage Register; but does not exclude members of the Royal Family from Part III of the 1949 Act (as amended, in particular by the Marriage Act 1994);[48] a reading of the 1949 Act which prevented The Prince of Wales and Mrs Parker Bowles from contracting a civil marriage would interfere with their rights under the European Convention on Human Rights ('the Convention'); and, section 3 of the Human Rights Act 1998, which requires legislation to be interpreted and given effect to in a way which is compliant with Convention rights, is a strong obligation which supports the conclusion that The Prince of Wales and Mrs Parker Bowles can rely on the provisions of Part III of the 1949 Act.

'A number of other points have also been mentioned in the caveats and I have investigated whether any of these amount to a legal impediment to marriage under the Marriage Act 1949. I am satisfied that none of these objections should obstruct the issue of a certificate.'

Of course, as Dr Stephen Cretney pointed out, the Registrar-General 'need not be, and is not at the present time, a lawyer'[49] (Len Cook was, in fact, a statistician, though a highly regarded one). His bald recital of the key objections and his interpretation of the 1949 Act added little to that of Lord Falconer. Indeed, on some points his argument was even more sparse: the only laws and customs that he mentioned as being preserved by the 1949 Act were the Royal Marriages Act and customs relating to the registration of royal marriages. This left open several crucial questions about the application of Parts II and III of the 1949 Act to royal marriages. If members of the royal family can take advantage of the provisions of Part III relating to non-Anglican ceremonies, are they also bound by those provisions that stipulate when a marriage will be void for non-compliance with the necessary formalities? And if that is the case for non-Anglican marriages, is it also the case for Anglican marriages? In other words, had the privileges accorded to members of the royal family in this context disappeared along with the restrictions?

Such issues—which are not mere matters of legal quibbling but which could ultimately lead to royal marriages being declared void—are precisely why it would have been preferable to deal with the question of royal marriages by a short and simple piece of legislation. Nonetheless, with dissenting voices such as Dr Stephen Cretney's having effectively been shouted down, the statement of the Registrar-General seemed to conclude the issue. One or two newspapers floated the possibility of objectors applying for judicial review of the Registrar-General's decision, but with little certainty that such a case could be brought, let alone succeed.[50] Only the *Mail* continued to express anxiety, revealing that there had been a 'secret contingency plan' for the wedding to take place in Scotland and commenting how this 'highlights the depth of unease over the threat of a serious legal challenge to the rearranged Windsor plans, and shows that even the highest royal aides doubted the legality of the wedding.'[51] The *Mail* continued, besides, to publish details from earlier government documents showing that Lord Falconer's predecessors had not thought a civil marriage possible for members of the royal family.[52]

There was, however, one final setback. It had been intended that the wedding would take place on Friday, April 8th, but following the death of the Pope on April 2nd the funeral was scheduled for the same date.[53] The civil ceremony accordingly took place on the 9th, and was followed by a blessing by the Archbishop of Canterbury in St George's Chapel at Windsor Castle.

Continuing doubts and a suspected cover-up

But doubts and dissatisfaction with Lord Falconer's advice remained. A year after the wedding, *The Times* ran the front-page headline 'An illegal marriage' next to a picture of Charles and Camilla. Inside, it reported how it had seen advice given to John Major's government to the effect that it was not possible for members of the royal family to marry in a civil wedding.[54] Two years later, the journalist Mark Jones requested information relating to Lord Falconer's interpretation of the law under the Freedom of Information Act 2000. This request was refused by the Ministry of Justice on the basis that such information was exempt from the 2000 Act by virtue of legal professional privilege. The Ministry of Justice also refused to confirm or deny whether the advice of the Attorney-General and the Solicitor-General, as Law Officers of the Crown, had been sought or given on the issue.

The Information Commissioner subsequently held that 'the public interest in maintaining the exemptions outweighs the public interest in disclosure.'[55]

While it was acknowledged by the Ministry of Justice that disclosing the content of legal advice could 'contribute to an open and transparent relationship between the government and the public' and 'ensure that the government are accountable for the decisions that they make', it was also noted that legal advice was 'likely to comment on negative and positive implications of a situation.' The implication was that making such advice available to the public would reduce the quality of the advice given, by encouraging legal advisors to include only the arguments in favour of a particular course of action.

Yet this hardly makes sense. One would of course expect legal advisors to canvass the strengths and weaknesses of opposing arguments. One would also expect them to indicate why they thought one particular set of arguments was stronger than the other. Far from giving ammunition to those who might want to mount a legal challenge, such advice, if sound, would demonstrate why such a challenge would be likely to fail—assuming, of course, that the government had actually followed the advice given in formulating its policy.

In deciding that the information should not be made public, the Information Commissioner noted the importance of 'informing the debate on the issue surrounding the marriage of the Heir to the Throne' but decided that the 'sensitivity and significance' of the information outweighed any public interest in disclosure. Yet one would expect that the significance of the decision would be a reason for, rather than against, disclosure. The allusion to the 'sensitivity' of the material is also problematic: from Lord Falconer's public statement it would appear that the ability of members of the royal family to marry in a civil ceremony rests on a simple matter of statutory interpretation, rather than anything personal to the parties themselves.

The second element of the Commissioner's decision concerned the refusal of the Ministry of Justice to confirm or deny whether the Law Officers had been consulted. Throughout the whole train of events, Lord Falconer and Clarence House insisted that advice had been taken from four separate sources. The identity of those sources has never been revealed. Whether they included the Law Officers must remain a matter of speculation. The Ministerial Code requires the Law Officers to 'be consulted in good time before the Government is committed to critical decisions involving legal considerations,' but both the content and the fact of their advice is not to be disclosed without their agreement.[56]

The Commissioner noted the level of debate in the media as well as in academic circles, adding, with considerable understatement, that 'the issue in this case could be considered to amount to a matter of significance in British constitutional history, given that it relates to the legality of the marriage of the Heir to the Throne.' On such a matter, he said, 'there would have been a widely-held assumption that the Government should, and would, have sought the advice of its most senior lawyers.' Were it to transpire that the government had not done so, this would of course 'raise important issues about the basis on which the Government satisfied itself that its interpretation of the relevant legislation was correct.'

Yet again, he held that the Ministry of Justice was justified in refusing to confirm or deny whether such advice had been sought, suggesting that disclosure of the kind sought might place inappropriate pressure on the government and the Law Officers themselves:

> 'If the government routinely disclosed the occasions on which the Law Officers had given advice, that could give rise to questions as to why they had not advised in other cases, thus creating pressure for them to advise in cases where their involvement is not justified.'

Were it to become routine, this might indeed be a concern,

but this hardly seems a reason for justifying the refusal to disclose information on a matter acknowledged to be of such significance. The Commissioner's suggestion that this was a 'constitutional matter' rather than one of government policy would in fact seem to be a justification *for* disclosure rather than the reverse.

The publication of the Commissioner's decision early in 2010 predictably led to a rash of headlines accusing the authorities of a cover-up and inviting speculation on the contents of Lord Falconer's advice. 'Prince Charles will take wedding "secret" to his grave,' declared the *Daily Telegraph* enigmatically.[57] As Michael Jones put it: 'if Falconer was so sure of his grounds, why is the Justice Ministry so strongly opposed to allowing the advice he took to be made public?'[58]

Happy news?

Even the happy news that Prince William was to wed Kate Middleton provided a further opportunity for the media to cast doubt on his father's marriage. 'It was not so simple for Charles,' ran one headline, above an article that recited the various problems that had bedevilled the Prince in the weeks leading up to the wedding.[59] The *Daily Mail* called on Charles to stand aside in favour of his son, noting the 'highly ambiguous position of his wife' given that '[t]he gravest doubts continue among some constitutional historians and lawyers over the validity of their marriage' and suggesting that Cabinet ministers 'were lent on to sanction this dubious marriage.'[60]

And a few days later a 'slip of the tongue' during an interview on the American chat-show *Dateline*—to the effect that his wife 'could be' queen when he succeeds to the throne—also attracted discussion. Most commentators pointed out that the wife of a king automatically becomes queen,[61] but the co-founder of the Diana Appreciation Society suggested that Camilla was not his wife: 'We think the wedding should never have been allowed. We don't think it was legal. We don't want him to be King.'[62]

But whatever criticisms can be levelled at the reasoning of Lord Falconer—and they are manifold—it seems clear that the marriage of the Prince of Wales is not now open to challenge. As noted above, it would, in theory, have been possible for the decision of the Registrar-General to have been challenged by means of judicial review. But no such challenge was ever brought, and the time limit for any such challenge has now long passed. Any marriage is also, in theory, open to challenge by those who would stand to benefit were it shown to be void. But in this case there is no one who could bring such a challenge. Finally, there is a strong presumption that a marriage that has been celebrated, apparently according to the prescribed rules, is valid.[63] Even if the marriage were ever to be challenged, this presumption would work in its favour.[64] The marriage of Prince Charles and the Duchess of Cornwall must, therefore, be regarded as impregnable.

But this does not mean that the arguments advanced by Lord Falconer and the Registrar-General were correct or even convincing. And, given that their arguments have implications for the rules that apply to royal marriages—and therefore for any members of the royal family who might marry in the future—they require detailed consideration.

Royal privileges and human rights

There were two key strands to the arguments advanced by Lord Falconer and the Registrar-General. The first was that the Marriage Act 1949 did, contrary to what had previously been thought, allow members of the royal family to marry in a civil ceremony in England and Wales. The reasons why the 1949 Act was framed in the way it was, and the clear intention of those responsible for drafting it that no change in the law applicable to members of the royal family was intended, have already been discussed, and Lord Falconer's dismissive comment that previous interpretations were 'over-cautious' does not provide convincing support for his alternative interpretation.

The second argument was that the Human Rights Act 1998 put this interpretation of the 1949 Act 'beyond doubt.'[65] Unfortunately, vague invocations of human rights are all too common, and reference to the Act may invite scepticism rather than offering reassurance. Though in popular imagination the Human Rights Act might well be a kind of 'magic wand' which need only be waved for the law to change, this is not the case in terms of law. It is therefore crucial to consider exactly how the Human Rights Act might apply to this particular case, and to members of the royal family more generally.

Lord Falconer's contention was, in essence, that even if the Marriage Act 1949 did not allow members of the royal family to marry in a civil ceremony, the requirements of the Human Rights Act dictated that it should be read as if it did. Distinct stages of legal reasoning are necessary in order to achieve this result. First, it needs to be shown that the current legislation (in this case the Marriage Act 1949) is in breach of the European Convention on Human Rights, which the Human Rights Act incorporated into English law. The finding of a violation is, however, only the first step. There are then two possible ways of dealing with such a violation. If it is possible to interpret the legislation in a manner that is compatible with the Convention, the decision-maker should do so. If, however, a compatible interpretation of the legislation is not possible, then the court's only option is to issue a declaration of incompatibility. Under this second route, the offending piece of legislation remains on the statute book with full legislative force until Parliament acts to amend the law. These issues need to be considered in relation to two separate questions: first, would there have been a violation of the European Convention if the Prince of Wales had been unable to marry Mrs Parker Bowles in a civil ceremony; and second, would there be a violation of the Convention if members of the royal family were limited to marrying in an Anglican ceremony?

The application of the Convention to Charles and Camilla

As noted above, in deciding whether an individual's rights under Article 12 have been breached, the question is whether the law operates 'in such a way or to such an extent that the very essence of the right is impaired.'[66] But is 'the essence of the right' to marry impaired if an individual is prevented from going through one particular form of marriage, to one particular person, in one particular part of the United Kingdom, as in this case Prince Charles was only prevented from going through a non-Anglican marriage with Camilla Parker Bowles in England and Wales, but was yet free to marry in other ways in other places?

Is there, for example, a right to marry in a particular form, if such a form is available to the general population? During the debates on the Human Rights Bill, concern was expressed that religious bodies might be forced be officiate at marriages of which they disapproved.[67] Assurances were given, however, that there would be no right to marry according to particular religious rites. As the then Home Secretary Jack Straw noted: 'article 12 does not include the right to marry according to a particular ceremony of one's choice.'[68] It should however be remembered that this argument rested on the assumption that civil marriage was available to all, and that this was suffi-cient to meet the UK's obligations under Article 12—the key issue under debate here.

If Charles and Camilla were truly barred from both a civil marriage (on account of his royal status) *and* a Church of England ceremony (on account of their being divorcees), it could reasonably be argued that no form of marriage was open to them. There is, though, a snag with this reasoning: were the couple actually barred from having a Church of England wedding? Clergy of the Church of England are not barred from celebrating the marriages of divorcees; instead, the relevant legislation merely provides that Anglican clergymen are not *obliged* to celebrate any such marriage, which is an important difference.

Although the Church of England's guidelines on the remarriage of divorced persons during the lifetime of their former spouses had been relaxed prior to 2005, they still included questions such as 'would the new marriage be likely to be a cause of hostile public comment or scandal' and 'would permitting the new marriage be tantamount to consecrating an old infidelity?'[69] Bearing those guidelines in mind, it is understandable that the Archbishop of Canterbury felt unable to conduct the marriage. Yet the vicar of Charles' local parish church in Gloucestershire, the Reverend John Wright, had in 2003 indicated that he would be willing to officiate at the marriages of divorcees, although he did acknowledge that this was not automatic. The *Daily Telegraph*'s comment was that 'St Mary's looks an increasingly attractive venue for a low-key royal wedding.'[70] The important point for our purposes is that a Church of England wedding was not an impossibility.

And of course it must be remembered that another, far simpler option was open to the couple. Over the border in Scotland, still part of the United Kingdom but with its own unique laws, Charles and Camilla could have married in either a civil or a religious ceremony. Scottish legislation on marriage makes no reference to members of the royal family, and the Church of Scotland allows the marriage of divorcees, so all legal modes of marriage would have been available to them. If Charles and Camilla had chosen to marry in Scotland, it might even have been possible for them to marry in a royal residence rather than in a register office: as in England and Wales, a range of places may be approved for the celebration of marriage, but, unlike the position south of the border, one-off approval can be obtained for a specific marriage.[71] Approval could have been sought for a marriage in the Prince of Wales' own residence of Birkhall, on the Balmoral estate in

Aberdeenshire, or elsewhere.

It is understandable that the heir to the throne might want a rather grander ceremony. But if these other options were legally available to the couple within the UK, it makes it very difficult to argue that the Marriage Act 1949 needed to be reinterpreted in order to bring it into compliance with Article 12 of the European Convention on Human Rights. Legislation need only be compatible with the Convention; it is not necessary for the law to promote human rights and freedom of choice to their fullest extent.[72] The extra costs that might have been incurred in travelling to Scotland would hardly have posed an obstacle in this particular case. And although the English courts have recently held limitations on the marriages of those subject to immigration control to be legally objectionable, the requirement for such people to give notice in specified places, perhaps to their personal inconvenience, did not come in for criticism.[73]

The application of the convention to royalty

But, even if the current law does not violate Article 12, might there be an argument that it violates Article 14? Article 14 prohibits discrimination on the basis of, amongst other things, birth, and the royal exclusion from non-Anglican forms of marriage is unarguably based solely on birth. And, importantly for the future, considering the case under Article 14 extends the debate beyond the issue of the remarriage of the Prince of Wales, since all members of the royal family are affected by the restriction in the Marriage Act 1949.

It does have to be borne in mind that Article 14 is not a free-standing provision, and that it only applies if an individual is discriminated against in relation to another of the rights set out in the Convention. But in this context that hurdle is easily met: it would be possible for a court to find that the law violated Article 14 on the basis that the marriages of members of the royal family were treated differently from those of the general public on account of their birth. Under the case-law of the Convention on Human Rights, a difference in treatment may only be justified if it is proportionate to a legitimate aim.[74] Is the bar on non-Anglican marriages for members of the royal family, then, intended to promote a legitimate aim? It could be argued that it is designed to ensure that members of the royal family are also members of the Church of England, and to impose restrictions on remarriage after divorce. Yet the sovereign alone is required to uphold the Church of England, and even he or she need not be a practising Anglican believer.[75] Even if it were thought desirable to maintain the prohibition on the monarch entering into any other form of marriage than an Anglican one, a bar on non-Anglican marriages for *all* royalty would hardly be a proportionate means of achieving this.

In any case, even if the restrictions were in fact proportionate to a legitimate aim, the fact that they can be so easily avoided by a trip to another legal jurisdiction within the UK undermines any argument that they serve a useful purpose. From this angle, the option of marriage in Scotland works in *favour* of the argument that the law as it currently stands violates the European Convention on Human Rights. If a case such as this ever came before an English court, it is likely that it would come to the view that there is no rational reason for preventing royals from marrying in a civil ceremony in England and Wales if they can do so elsewhere in the UK.

And so these observations get us over the first hurdle: it is likely (though not certain) that the Marriage Act 1949 would be judged as incompatible with Article 14 of the European Convention on Human Rights. But this is not simply the end of the matter: it would then need to be decided whether or not the Act could be interpreted in a way that is consistent with the Convention, or whether fresh legislation would be needed to replace it.

It is clear that the Human Rights Act may require the courts to adopt an 'unnatural' or strained interpretation in order to achieve compatibility with the Convention. The courts may even need to read words into a statute in order to ensure that it is compliant. Let us remind ourselves of the precise terms of the provision which would need to be reinterpreted, s.79(5) of the Marriage Act 1949:

> 'Nothing in this Act is intended to affect any law or custom relating to marriages of the Royal Family.'[76]

This is rather uncompromising material to work with, especially given the quite definite way in which it has been interpreted in the past. Undeterred, both Lord Falconer and the Registrar-General asserted in the most positive terms that the 'clear' and 'natural' meaning of this clause was to allow members of the royal family to marry in a civil ceremony. Their insistence on this point in fact impeded their ability to make a convincing argument that the section should be interpreted in a manner consistent with the Convention, since it precluded any suggestion as to which new words might be read into the Marriage Act 1949 to render it compliant.

To supply this deficiency, let us think about what words could conceivably be read into the section to ensure that the law does not violate the rights of members of the royal family. It could, perhaps, state that 'Nothing in Parts I, II or IV of this Act is intended to affect any law or custom relating to marriages of the Royal Family.' But this immediately raises discrepancies: Part III, dealing with non-Anglican marriages, contains a section setting out the circumstances in which a marriage will be void for a failure to comply with the law; Part II contains a similar provision to deal with Anglican marriages. If Part III applied to members of the royal family, but Part II did not, there would be the risk that a member of the royal family who married in a civil ceremony could find their marriage to be void for a failure to comply with the law while one who married in an Anglican ceremony would not, regardless of the extent of their failure to comply with the law. In short, discrimination would continue, even if in a modified form. One might imagine that members of the royal family would receive the best available legal advice and would never be in any danger of failing to comply with the legal requirements, but this book would have been considerably shorter had that been the case.

An alternative would be to rewrite the section so that it read 'Nothing in Parts I or IV of this Act is intended to affect any law or custom relating to marriages of the Royal Family.' This would preserve the effect of the Royal Marriages Act and the current practices relating to the registration of royal marriages, while placing royals on the same footing as everyone else in terms of the formalities to be observed. But it is quite clear that Lord Falconer did not envisage such a reinterpretation, since he was quoted in the *Mail on Sunday* as saying that there was 'no need for Royals to post banns before getting married or obtaining a licence.'[77] Was he suggesting that Anglican royal marriages should be treated differently from other forms of marriage in this regard (which, as explained above, would still violate the Convention)? Or was he implying that members of the royal family should continue to be exempt from both of the annulling clauses of the Marriage Act 1949—in short, that they are entitled to special treatment on account of their birth? There is clearly a good case for holding that, under the Human Rights Act, members of the royal family should have the right to marry in any ceremony that is available to the general public, and should not be discriminated against on account of their birth. The attractions of that argument are, however, somewhat diminished if at the same time it is argued that members of the royal family enjoy the privilege of ignoring the legal requirements with impunity on account of their birth. Combining royal privileges and human rights in this manner is tricky and self-contradictory.[78] As the comedian David Mitchell was to put it in the *Observer*:

> 'The monarchy is overwhelmingly, gloriously, intentionally unfair—that's the point. The defining unfairness is that you

have to be a member of that family to be king or queen; fringe unfairnesses like their not being able to marry Catholics or men having priority in the line of succession are irrelevant in that context.'[79]

So the process of reading words into the statute to ensure that it complies with the Convention is no easy matter. Change one element, and other parts are immediately called into question. This is why courts will often issue a simple declaration that a particular piece of legislation is incompatible rather than overstep their role by suggesting how it should be reinterpreted. As Dr Aileen Kavanagh, a human rights and constitutional law expert and Fellow of St Edmund Hall, Oxford, has correctly pointed out, 'mere linguistic possibility' is not the sole criterion for the courts when deciding whether legislation can be interpreted in a way that is compatible with the Convention, and 'the courts will also take account of the possible consequences of such an interpretation.'[80] Broad questions of national policy, especially when they touch on matters of constitutional importance, are matters for the legislature, rather than for a court, to decide. Still less, one might add, are they matters for an individual office-holder such as a Lord Chancellor to decide.

The implications of invoking the Human Rights Act do not stop there. The bar to members of the royal family marrying according to non-Anglican rites was not the only part of the law to discriminate against them. Why, one might ask, were Lord Falconer and the Registrar-General so sure that the Royal Marriages Act remained good law? They were both, we might recall, happy to note in their official statements that the Marriage Act 1949 *preserved* the Royal Marriages Act, without either raising an eyebrow at its discriminatory provisions that affect the very capacity of members of the royal family to marry without the monarch's consent.[81] Unlike the bar on entering into a non-Anglican marriage in England and Wales, these apply however and wherever in the world the marriage takes place. It can hardly be justified as being a proportionate means of achieving a legitimate aim, especially if its scope is as wide as is feared, yet both Lord Falconer and the Registrar-General ignored this fact. As various commentators pointed out at the time, other aspects of the laws relating to royal marriage might also be vulnerable to challenge. According to Professor David Feldman of the University of Cambridge, the Human Rights Act 'could be used to challenge the constitutional foundation stones of the monarchy'—the Act of Settlement itself.[82]

To sum up this detailed look at the human rights angle, although there is a good case to be made in favour of the argument that not allowing members of the royal family to marry in a civil ceremony in England and Wales would violate the European Convention on Human Rights, it is far less clear that the disputed provision can be interpreted in a way that would render it compatible with the Convention. It is much more likely that primary legislation would be required before the law could safely be said to allow such a marriage. To claim otherwise is to ignore the Convention's history, purpose and context. It is clear that the reasons put forward by Lord Falconer and the Registrar-General were deeply flawed. Complicated and highly contentious legal issues concerning statutory interpretation and human rights were reduced to vague and simplistic assertions. The way that genuine doubts were dealt with certainly did not enhance the public standing of either the Human Rights Act or of the law in general. The public were left with the mistaken impression that mere invocation of the Human Rights Act could effect fundamental alterations to the law without discussion, and that long-standing legal assumptions could be overturned without legislation, court decision or even a convincing argument. Though Charles and Camilla's marriage cannot now be challenged, it is despite, rather than because of, Lord Falconer and New Labour's mishandling. The law governing royal marriage today, in the wake of these events, is less certain than before, especially given that there is also a compelling argument that the Royal Marriages Act—and, no less so, the Act of Settlement—also violate the rights laid down in the Convention.

The next royal civil marriage

The statements of Lord Falconer and the Registrar-General, then, leave the law on royal marriages in a state of considerable—and highly undesirable—uncertainty. One difficulty is the task of deciding upon the legal effect of a marriage that does not comply with the required formalities. If it is accepted that the *status quo* after Charles and Camilla's marriage is that the Marriage Act 1949 applies to members of the royal family in exactly the same way as it applies to the general population, then future royal marriages may be vulnerable to being annulled for non-compliance with the stipulated preliminaries. If any member of the royal family were now to marry in an Anglican ceremony assuming that they were still exempt from observing the preliminaries laid down by statute (such as the need for banns or a licence), as had always been the case, their marriages could be vulnerable to challenge.[83]

Let us for a moment imagine a hypothetical situation where a royal personage marries in an Anglican ceremony that fails to comply with the statutory requirements. If he or she were to die intestate and without children, a relative might wish to challenge the validity of the marriage and so stand to inherit property which would otherwise have passed to the spouse. If the Marriage Act 1949 applies to royalty, then a court might reasonably hold the marriage to be void.

What then if our hypothetical situation were to involve a civil ceremony rather than an Anglican one? If the person marrying were relatively distant from the throne, a court hearing a challenge to the marriage would be most likely to sidestep all the issues discussed above and simply interpret the meaning of the words 'Royal Family' in their narrowest possible sense. In other words, the individual in question would not be a member of the royal family for the purpose of the Marriage Act 1949, and would be entitled to marry in any way open to the general population. The courts, after all, have shown themselves to be unwilling to overturn marriages entered into by couples after the due preliminaries have been observed, especially when both parties have genuinely believed that their marriage is valid.

More complex questions would arise, though, if the civil marriage were of a senior royal, close to the throne. The court would again err on the side of upholding the marriage if possible, but what grounds would it be able to find to justify the marriage's validity against a legal challenge? With a marriage involving a senior royal, the court would be unable to interpret the meaning of the words 'Royal Family' in the Marriage Act 1949 in a way that excluded them, and would need instead to look at the detailed provisions of the legislation. In the best-case scenario, interpreting the Marriage Act 1949 in the light of the Human Rights Act the court might decide that it was possible to read words into the 1949 Act to make it compatible with the European Convention. Lord Falconer's written statement is positively unhelpful in this respect, in that it insisted that the 'clear' and 'natural' interpretation of the wording of the 1949 Act was that it *did* allow royal civil marriage. This assertion would make it hard to argue that there were any need to read new words into the Act to achieve this interpretation. Still, the complicated knock-on effects of any new wording notwithstanding, a court might possibly still uphold our senior royal's civil marriage as valid by doing just that. We cannot, regrettably, be sure; nor is it possible to predict precisely which words the court would read into the Act.

In the worst-case scenario, however, a court might declare it impossible to find the Marriage Act 1949 compatible with the Human Rights Act. The court would then need to address the question of whether a member of the royal family, by exchanging vows before a registrar, had married in a way which had been available to the general public before 1754 and which had continued to be available to royals after that time.

I have already shown that before 1754 the only form of marriage accepted by the law was one celebrated before an Anglican clergyman. A simple exchange of vows—such as would have occurred in our hypothetical senior royal's civil ceremony—would not in itself have been regarded as a marriage. To frame eighteenth-century distinctions in modern legal language is almost impossible, but the most likely outcome is that a simple exchange of vows without an Anglican clergyman being present would be a 'non-marriage'. Such a ceremony has no legal status at all, and the parties to it would be treated no differently from a couple who have lived together without marrying.

Why would it not be possible for the court to salvage such a ceremony by resort to the reassuring words of the Marriage Act 1949 that a marriage is only void if the parties 'knowingly and wilfully' fail to comply with certain stipulated formalities? The answer is simply that if the marriages of members of the royal family fall outside the statutory scheme, then their validity—or otherwise—cannot be tested by reference to the statute. Nor would the subsequent blessing in church of such a civil marriage make any difference to the court's decision. The standard form of the Church of England's *Order for Prayer and Dedication after a Civil Marriage* deliberately involves no exchange of vows, 'to avoid any suggestion that the initial form had not created a valid marriage.'[84] So although a blessing would involve the presence of an Anglican clergyman, the other vital element, the exchange of vows, would be missing.

So, in the worst-case scenario of our hypothetical future civil marriage of a senior royal, the outcome would be that a couple who had assumed they were married would find that they were merely cohabitants in the eyes of the law. This would have serious consequences for the rights of any children that they might have—who would not be entitled to succeed to any title or, indeed, the throne.

To return finally to a real-life civil marriage of a senior royal, that of Prince Charles to Camilla Parker Bowles, I have already made the observation that, years after the event, there is nobody in a position to challenge its validity, and that it is therefore impregnable. But this might not be the case for any future royal marriages conducted on the assumption that members of the royal family are now entitled to marry in a non-Anglican ceremony. Some such marriages have already taken place, although none would appear to be vulnerable to challenge. In 2006, for example, Lord Nicholas Windsor and Paola Doimi de Frankopan went through a civil ceremony of marriage in a London register office. In this case there is no doubt as to the marital status of the couple, who two weeks later went through a Catholic ceremony at the Church of St Stephen of the Abyssinians in the Vatican City,[85] putting the validity of their marriage beyond question. At least two relatives of the Queen have married in purely civil ceremonies since 2005. Benjamin Lascelles married in 2009 at the family home of the Lascelles, Harewood House, which is licensed for civil marriage,[86] but was born before the marriage of his parents and so would be regarded as being outside the scope of the term 'Royal Family' in the 1949 Act.[87] In 2008, Charles Liddell-Grainger married at Westminster register office. Any challenge to his marriage would fail if a court were simply to decide that the term 'Royal Family' in the Marriage Act 1949 should be limited to those who bear a royal title, leaving wider kin to marry in any way available to the general population. In any case, as noted in the case of Charles and Camilla, any marriage, royal included, entered into after the prescribed formalities have been observed and under the authority of a registrar must be presumed to be valid.

But there is a whole generation of young royals at varying distances to the throne who are likely to be marrying in the next few years, and, as Dr Stephen Cretney has commented, 'the marriage laws now in force contain defects which create uncertainty, embarrassment, and even hardship without achieving any compensating policy objective.'[88] Had the complexity and limitations of the law been acknowledged by New Labour in 2005, legislation could have been passed to resolve the position, and there would have been no need for speculation about how a court might interpret the law in case of challenge, or how the Human Rights Act might apply to centuries-old statutes. I make no apology to the reader for the complexity of the arguments presented in this chapter: there is no point in trying to pretend that matters are simpler than they are, and the events of 2005 raised far more questions than were ever answered at the time. At the same time, there is no excuse for continuing with a set of laws that are so riddled with uncertainty. The position should be clarified for the sake of future royal marriages, and the final chapter will look at how that might be achieved.

chapter 6

The Future of our Marriage Laws

TO RETURN to the idea of royal marriages being 'a brilliant edition of a universal fact', it is clear that, in legal terms at least, this is now further from the truth than it has ever been. The Act of Settlement of 1701 still dictates that those who marry a Catholic forfeit their right to the throne; the Royal Marriages Act of 1772 still requires a whole host of persons to obtain the consent of the sovereign in order to be capable of marrying; and members of the royal family have been exempted from compliance with the usual formalities of marriage since the law was first put on a statutory footing in 1753.

By contrast, all other members of the community have a much greater choice of where and whom they may marry. Since 1994 the choice of venues has widened from religious buildings and register offices to any approved premises.[1] The highest court in the land has declared that a restrictive set of formalities applicable to individuals subject to immigration control who wish to marry outside the Anglican Church are contrary to the European Convention on Human Rights.[2] In a similar vein, the Court of Appeal has held that limiting to those over the age of 21 the ability to sponsor a spouse's entry to this country contravenes the human rights of those involved.[3] For everyone other than members of the royal family, it is clear, considerable importance is attached to the exercise of choice in the context of marriage.

It is worth re-emphasizing that the current restrictions on members of the royal family were not intended to create such a divide between them and the rest of the population. Indeed, the current legislation, when passed, would not have appeared out of the ordinary—and not because members of the royal family were subject to greater restrictions than today, but because the general population were. So, while the fact that any member of the royal family marrying a Catholic forfeits the right to inherit the Crown appears discriminatory to modern eyes, at the time that it was introduced it was no harsher than the laws that prevented Catholics from worshipping openly, sitting in Parliament, holding land, entering the legal profession, and more besides.

The same is true of the requirement that the sovereign give consent to the marriage of members of the royal family. Given that this raises the possibility that two people who love each other may be prevented from entering into an otherwise legal union, it is clearly problematic now that marriages are entered into for personal rather than dynastic reasons. Yet when Parliament introduced this provision in 1772, the marriage of any minor without parental consent would, in certain circumstances at least, be void.[4] The courts of the day were quite happy to uphold clauses in wills and settlements making financial provision dependent on any marriage going ahead only with the consent of a named person.[5] The familiar image of a young man asking the consent of his sweetheart's father was not always just a mere matter of courtesy, but in many cases was essential to the marriage going ahead.

The disputed rules which today govern *how* members of the royal family may marry have a similar history. When the general law of marriage was first put on a statutory basis in 1753, the change did little more than formalize the existing requirements of the canon law of the Church of England. Royalty, despite being exempted from the new legislation, were thus able to marry in exactly the same ways as members of the general population. They were, nevertheless, protected from those elements of the legislation which declared that a marriage would be void if certain formalities were not observed. In time, though, this princely privilege became a restriction, as new modes of marrying (for example in a civil ceremony) were made available to the population as a whole but consistently not extended to members of the royal family.

The increasingly archaic nature of the rules regulating royal marriages, when compared to those of non-royals, has been apparent for some time: the provision rendering general marriages void if celebrated without parental consent was modified in 1823, and since then the absence of consent has no longer rendered a marriage void;[6] the suite of laws that discriminated against Catholics began to be dismantled in the late eighteenth century and were finally repealed in 1829; and since 1836 civil marriages, and those according to non-Anglican religious rites, have been available to the general population.

The fact that royalty were not entitled to marry in a civil ceremony barely merited comment in the days when few of the population as a whole took this option. Early perceptions of civil marriage were highly negative, its operation tied up with the Poor Laws and, worse, the workhouse. Civil marriage was 'clerically denounced as fit only for infidels, and popularly regarded as not genuine marriage.'[7] Even by the start of the twentieth century, only 15 per cent of those marrying chose to do so in a civil ceremony. In contrast, by its close, civil marriage had become the norm, with 64 per cent of marriages taking this form. When the second marriage of the Prince of Wales was under discussion in 2005, a common and understandable reaction was 'if everyone else can get married in a civil ceremony, why can't he?'

The case for reform

Having reviewed the three sets of rules that apply to the marriages of members of the royal family, it is clear that each had its genesis in very specific historical circumstances. The Act of Settlement was rooted in the discriminatory political climate of the day, while the Royal Marriages Act was a response to a very particular problem and was rooted in personalities as much as, if not more than, principles. The exemption from the general law came about rather differently, and little if any thought was given to the consequences.

Officials have long acknowledged that the law relating to members of the royal family is outdated. The desirability of reform is hard to dispute. The provisions relating to Catholics have been described, with good reason, as 'deeply offensive.'[8] There is widespread public support for change: in 2009 a poll carried out by the BBC found that 81 per cent of those surveyed would be happy for the heir to the throne to be allowed to marry a Catholic.[9] As one commentator noted of the last set of debates, 'no-one seemed willing to attempt any reasoned defence of the status quo.'[10]

In any case, quite apart from the discriminatory and restrictive nature of the current statutory provisions, the law relating to royal marriages hardly forms a coherent code.

First, there are a number of loopholes and inconsistencies. A person who marries a Catholic forfeits his or her entitlement to succeed to the throne, but if a member of the royal family marries someone who subsequently converts to Catholicism the succession is unaffected. When the Duchess of Kent became a Catholic in 1994, her husband retained his place in the succession. He was, admittedly, a rather remote eighteenth in line at the time, but there is nothing to prevent the spouse of any future heir apparent from converting to Rome.[11] Yet contradictorily, once an individual's place in the succession has been forfeited on account of marriage to a Catholic, it does not re-emerge should their spouse be received into the Anglican Church.

The introduction of civil partnerships raises another intriguing discrepancy. Despite its twenty-seven schedules amending virtually every piece of legislation that made any reference to 'marriage' or 'spouse', the Civil Partnerships Act 2004 made no reference to either the Act of Settlement or the Royal Marriages Act. A member of the royal family does not, therefore, need the consent of the sovereign in order to enter into a same-sex partnership. Were the partner in question to be a Catholic—a remote contingency, perhaps—the royal's place in the succession would be unaffected.[12]

Secondly, each of the pieces of legislation we have examined has a different effect, a different geographical application, and affects different persons. So, under the Act of Settlement the marriage of a member of the royal family to a Catholic is not void, but excludes that person from the succession, whereas a marriage that takes place in contravention of the Royal Marriages Act is absolutely void from the start. With regard to the territorial scope of the different pieces of legislation, it is clear that both the Act of Settlement and the Royal Marriages Act apply to marriages wherever celebrated: it is not possible to evade them by marrying overseas.[13] By contrast, there is no specific provision preventing members of the royal family from validly marrying in a civil ceremony outside England and Wales, and many, as listed previously, have done so.[14]

As to the knotty question of to whom these different pieces of legislation in practice apply, the Royal Marriages Act is the most specific, stating that it applies to all descendants of George II other than the issue of princesses who have married into foreign families.[15] But marriage into a foreign family does not, of course, affect the rights of succession to the throne, so the Act of Settlement may still apply to those who are no longer subject to the Royal Marriages Act.

This leads on to a third problem. Not only are there obvious contradictions in the legislation, but numerous uncertainties exist about the scope of its detailed provisions. We have already seen how officials in the 1950s disagreed about the scope of the Royal Marriages Act; indeed, files in the National Archives contain a draft announcement to the effect that 'as the Act is so uncertain in its application... the time has come when it should be repealed.'[16]

Perhaps surprisingly, still uncertain is what is actually meant by 'members of the Royal Family' in the Marriage Act 1949 and its predecessors. The marriage legislation enacted in the 1753, 1836 and 1949 Acts uses this deceptively simple wording, but it should by now have become clear that even such an apparently inconspicuous phrase can be interpreted in a myriad of ways. Who, in short, is exempt from complying with the general law of marriage—or, less favourably, is unable to take advantage of those methods of marriage introduced by statute? 'Family' is of course a word capable of a variety of meanings, and the word 'royal' was not defined in any of the general pieces of legislation dealing with the formalities required for a valid marriage.

But it would appear that 'royal family' was thought to have a broad ambit in this context. As we have seen, when Lady Iris Mountbatten married in 1941, the Law Officers took the view that she was a member of the royal family for this purpose, and that she was therefore not allowed to marry in a Catholic ceremony. As a great-grandchild of Queen Victoria, she was no remoter a relation than Prince Sigvard of Sweden, who married in a civil ceremony at Caxton Hall in London in 1934.[17] Yet she bore no royal title, and fell outside the ambit of the 'royal family' as defined by the George V Settlement of 1917, which limited its scope to the monarch, his children and grandchildren.[18] It is difficult to formulate a rule that would distinguish the one case from the other, especially if all the descendants of Princess Sophia are, perhaps unbeknownst to themselves, British citizens. It would of course be absurd if members of foreign royal families were to be barred from a civil marriage in England and Wales simply on the basis that they were remotely related to the British royal family, or if those who have already married in this way should suddenly find their marriages being challenged in court.[19] But then it would be equally absurd if members of foreign royal families who happened to be descendants of George II should find their marriages to be invalid because they had not obtained the consent of the British monarch—yet that remains a real, if remote, possibility under the Royal Marriages Act.[20]

And, as we have seen, the events of 2005 raise further questions about the content of the rules that currently apply to members of the royal family. The *Guardian* posed the question: 'if the Human Rights Act applies to the Marriage Act, then why should it not apply equally to the explicitly discriminatory provisions of the Act of Settlement?'[21] The same point was raised by Lord Lamont of Lerwick in the course of debates in Parliament.[22] As one academic commentator noted, 'it might be determined that there should be no obstacle to their human rights and the archaic laws can be held to be repealed by inference.'[23] On that interpretation, all of the rules discussed in this book have simply vanished, as if by magic. This, though, is not how the law works.

The case for reform—whether to repeal, amend, or simply clarify the law—is a compelling one. But the one point that emerges most clearly from the behind-the-scenes discussions among officials in the twentieth century is the depth of the reluctance to do anything about the law in this area. When general reform was being discussed in 1948, it was suggested that '[t]he present time would seem ill-chosen for an alteration affecting Royal Marriages.'[24] Four years later, when the deficiencies of the Royal Marriages Act were being discussed, the Lord Chancellor took the view that 'the best course would be to do nothing unless and until any practical need for action arose.'[25] When, however, the constraints imposed by the Royal Marriages Act became a pressing issue, with Princess Margaret's possible marriage to Townsend being mooted, it was felt that 'at present the objections to taking action seem to outweigh the advantages.'[26] Once that prospect had receded, it was acknowledged that ministers 'will probably be reluctant to tackle this problem otherwise than under the pressure of an immediate need such as might have arisen in October.'[27] In short, in the absence of a crisis, reform has been regarded as unnecessary, and in the presence of a crisis any change has been deemed too difficult.

Successive governments, even those that have effected dramatic changes in other spheres, have been reluctant to engage in legislation relating to the monarchy. As one professor of constitutional law has pointed out, New Labour was always 'at pains to stress that its long and substantial shopping list of constitutional reforms would not affect the Crown.'[28]

Proposals for reform

Despite the striking absence of any government-sponsored reform, there have in recent years been a number of MPs from all points of the political spectrum who have introduced private members' bills on the monarchy. Lord Archer of Weston-super-Mare made two attempts at reform, in 1997 and 1998, while in 2001 Kevin McNamara MP introduced the more wide-ranging (and luxuriantly named) Treason Felony, Act of Settlement and Parliamentary Oath Bill.

In 2005 there were no fewer than three bills on the topic, one in the House of Lords and two in the House of Commons,[29] while in 2007 John Gummer MP (a convert to Catholicism) introduced the self-explanatory Catholics (Prevention of Discrimination) Bill. Most recently, the Royal Marriages and Succession to the Crown Bill 2009 was introduced by the Liberal MP Dr Evan Harris and attracted considerable attention in the media.

All of these bills have had at their core the repeal or reform of both the Royal Marriages Act and of the restrictions contained in the Act of Settlement relating to marriages with Catholics. None, however, have attempted to deal with the issue of the form that royal marriages take. Given the obstacles that lie in the path of any such bill ever making it on to the statute book, most were used as a means of drawing attention to the issues rather than with serious legislative intent. Even though five hours of wide-ranging debate were devoted to the Royal Marriages and Succession to the Crown Bill 2009, it failed to proceed to a second reading.[30] This was largely because of what can only be described as a filibustering speech by the then Justice Secretary, Jack Straw, who

talked about the Smethwick election of 1964 and his gradu-
ation in 1967 before going back to Parliamentary debates from
1861 about the Irish peasantry and throwing in a few of the
more comprehensible lines of T.S. Eliot for good measure.
Since he was still talking at the end of the time allotted for the
debate on the second reading, any further discussion had to
be adjourned until a later date, and the Bill was subsequently
dropped.[31]

What is noticeable, however, is that virtually no one was
willing to make a principled argument for the retention of the
current law. The arguments advanced against reforming legislation have largely focused on practical issues, and essentially
fall into three camps: first, that there is no need to legislate
because the rules have no immediate discriminatory effect;[32]
secondly, that even if there is a need to legislate, any legislation dealing with important constitutional issues would be
extremely complex and would therefore need time;[33] and,
thirdly, that the government has other priorities for reform
and cannot spend time on members of the royal family.[34]

Yet, as Lord Dubs pointed out when introducing the
Succession to the Crown Bill in 2005, '[t]he easiest time
to legislate is when there are no personal implications for
individual members of the royal family.'[35] The complexities
raised by royal marriages are hardly more taxing than those
that a government has to face when passing other pieces of
legislation, and far more time has been devoted to far less
important issues.

That said, it is perfectly understandable that successive
governments should have shied away from addressing the Act
of Settlement. Dr Stephen Cretney has described the current
provisions relating to the religion of the sovereign as 'impossible to reconcile with 21st century attitudes to discrimination
based on ethnicity, gender, class or religion,' but acknowledged
the difficulty in reform given the fact that 'the importance
of preserving the link between the monarchy and Protes-
tantism is a matter on which strong feeling has been only too

apparent in some parts of the United Kingdom within the recent past.'[36] Throughout the debates on the various private members' bills mentioned above, it was the provisions of the Act of Settlement that attracted the most serious discussion, with the few who commented on the Royal Marriages Act dismissing it with such terms as 'ludicrous' and 'absurd'.

It is almost inevitable that still broader questions would be raised about the role of the monarchy in modern society should any bill relating only to the marriages of members of the royal family be introduced. At the time of the abdication crisis, for example, one MP proposed that the Crown should be abolished altogether.[37] Admittedly, the motion was defeated by the enormous margin of 398—with only five MPs voting in favour—but it illustrates that fears about wider grievances being raised would not be groundless. The risk that debates on the law applicable to members of the royal family would provide opportunities for republicans was adverted to by at least one MP in 2009.[38]

The way forward

An alternative way to achieve much-needed reform could be arrived at by inserting into a more general reform of marriage law a clause confirming that members of the royal family have the right to marry according to any form available to the general population. There are, in fact, good reasons for enacting such a reform independently of the position of members of the royal family.

The preliminaries required for all non-Anglican marriages have changed little since their introduction in 1836. Posting details of intended marriages on the notice board of the register office is hardly an efficient way of bringing them to public attention. Use of the internet would be a far more effective way of ensuring that any person who had a legitimate reason to object to a marriage going ahead learned of it in good time. The preliminaries for Anglican marriages have an even longer history, banns having been used to publicize intended marriages since the twelfth century and licences since the sixteenth. Back in 2002, the General Synod of the Church of England did in fact approve a new system of joint state and ecclesiastical preliminaries.[39] But to date no further steps have been taken towards the creation of a universal set of preliminaries for all marriages—something that has been under consideration since the early nineteenth century.

Other distinctions between Anglican and non-Anglican marriages also remain: there is, for example, no exact civil equivalent of the Archbishop of Canterbury's special licence. Had there been, the Prince of Wales might well have been able to marry in Windsor Castle as originally planned. The fact that the range of places that can be licensed for marriage is now so wide raises questions about the utility of the remaining restrictions. One possibility would be to move to a system such as that which operates in other jurisdictions where, as long as the person who conducts the ceremony has authority to do so, it matters not where the actual ceremony takes place. Such a reform was proposed as long ago as 2002[40] but never enacted.[41] It does, however, have a number of merits, not least that of allowing couples to personalize their marriage ceremony to a far greater extent. The Conservative Party has consistently spoken of its desire to encourage marriage, and a change of this kind is likely to be far more effective than modest tax incentives.

Liberalising the rules on where a marriage may take place would also enable more couples to marry in their own place of worship. At present, the ability of couples—other than those belonging to the Church of England or the Quaker or Jewish faiths—to celebrate their marriage in their local place of worship depends on whether it has been certified for religious worship *and* registered for marriage. This results in a number of anomalies: although there are over 1 million Muslims in England and Wales, only 162 mosques in England—and two in Wales—are registered for marriage.[42] For many couples from religious minorities, the only legal option is to marry in a civil ceremony and then have a religious ceremony.

Another oddity of the current law is that those marrying in civil ceremonies—or in religious ceremonies other than those according to Anglican, Jewish or Quaker rites—must repeat certain words that are laid down in statute. It makes sense to have such set words by which the bride and the groom declare that there is no impediment to their union and that they accept each other as husband and wife: there are many other ways in which the ceremony can be personalised. But there is, rather oddly, no requirement that the crucial vows be exchanged in a language that the parties understand: the only current concession to linguistic plurality is that a Welsh translation is available, though there are few Welsh monoglots.

Reforms are also necessary to address some of the uncertainties that bedevil the current general law. Back in 1973, a 'sound marriage law' was described as one that ensured 'that the status of those who marry shall be established with certainty so that doubts do not arise, either in the minds of the parties or in the community, about who is married and who is not.'[43] As it now stands, the law does not always achieve that very basic objective. Increasing religious and cultural diversity has meant that there have been a number of cases in which couples did not appreciate the need to comply with certain formal requirements in order to marry. These couples had all gone through a ceremony of marriage that complied with the rites laid down by their religion, and had lived together in the belief that they were married under English law. In some cases the courts managed to find reasons for upholding these marriages, but others unions were consigned to the non-status of 'non-marriage.'[44] There is some evidence to suggest that an increasing number of marriages are being entered into outside the framework laid down by the law—thus depriving the parties of the protection of English law should the relationship subsequently break down.[45]

There may be those who would argue that reforms to the law of marriage would be just as irrelevant as reforms to the laws affecting members of the royal family. It is a familiar theme that marriage is in decline in twenty-first century Britain. In fact, although the number of marriages has fallen since the 1970s, the decline is by no means as precipitous as has often been claimed. The number of marriages in 1972, the year against which subsequent figures are inevitably measured by the media, was particularly high on account of the large number of remarriages that took place in the wake of reforms to the law of divorce the previous year. Also, the annual figures published by the Office for National Statistics on the number of marriages taking place in England and Wales do not include the marriages of residents that take place overseas, for example on a beach in the Caribbean or on the Indian subcontinent. If these overseas marriages were included, the marriage statistics would instantly shoot up by some twenty-five percent, yet there is no official record of such marriages at all, since there is no requirement that the marriage be registered once the happy couple return to this country. Requiring couples to do so would provide much better information about the size and make-up of the married population, as well as change the atmosphere in which reporting on the apparent decline in marriage is conducted.

One of the most startling aspects of the changes proposed by the New Labour governments of 1997-2010 was the idea that they were to be achieved by delegated legislation, under the Regulatory Reform Act 2001. If Parliament wants to send a message about the significance of marriage in the twenty-first century, a debate on the floor of the House would be the ideal opportunity.

Certain minor reforms to marriage law have in fact been proposed in recent times. Tucked away in the Protection of Freedoms Bill, introduced in February 2011, was a clause removing the time restrictions on when marriages can take place. There have been indications of governmental intentions to abolish the rules requiring people subject to immigration control to obtain a certificate of approval before they marry. Rather than dealing with such matters by discrete pieces of legislation, it would be preferable to have reform that addressed at least some of the broader problems with the current law.

Such legislation could then include a clause confirming the validity of any royal marriages that had taken place since 2005 or, more subtly, simply exclude any mention of members of the royal family at all and so include them by default. It could also state that the provisions of the Royal Marriages Act should cease to have effect. Vernon Bogdanor, describing the Royal Marriages Act as 'absurd', has suggested that it could be restricted to the descendants of George VI 'or, better still, simply [to] the first five people in the line of succession.'[46] The first of these proposals would currently limit the application of the Act to fewer than two dozen people, though that number would inevitably grow and in future years new legislation would be needed to limit its scope once more; the latter proposal overlooks the fact that a person's place in the succession fluctuates over time. When Princess Margaret wanted to marry Peter Townsend, she was third in line to the throne; by the time of her death she was tenth. Conversely, it is conceivable that an individual might enter the 'top five' having previously married outside the scope of the amended Act, so rendering it less effective. But here is not the place to debate the pros and cons of details which ought to be decided by Parliament.

In the twenty-first century the brilliance of royal weddings has perhaps been overtaken by ever more lavish celebrity weddings. Those who may one day occupy a genuine throne are less likely than pop stars and footballers to incorporate ersatz versions into their wedding ceremony. But as long as Britain retains its monarchy, royal marriages remain of considerable public importance. For too long 'our happy ostrich-like national characteristics', as the Lord Chancellor Lord Kilmuir put it in the 1950s, have led to reform being deferred.[47] A responsible government is one that legislates for future contingencies as well as present problems.

Author's Note and Acknowledgments

I would like to thank all those who have provided advice, information and encouragement for this book. Stephen, Eileen and Trevor read the entire book in draft and gave very helpful feedback. Frances and Keith at Warwick Books were invaluable in organizing a launch and promoting the book before it was even in print. Christine Reynolds of Westminster Abbey Library kindly provided details from the abbey's marriage registers. Mike Goldmark of Goldmark Gallery in Uppingham very generously gave permission to use Gillray's delightfully bawdy and perfectly illustrative *The Fall of Phaeton* in the cover illustration. Jon Foster-Smith of Shine Design sacrificed what ought to have been a relaxing weekend to create the cover image from the original print.

This book has required the use of a large number of royal and aristocratic titles, and there will, inevitably, be instances where I have used an incorrect form. I offer my apologies in advance, and would be glad to be told of these and any others errors so that they can be corrected for future editions.

Bibliography

Anderson, O., 'The Incidence of Civil Marriage in Victorian England and Wales' (1975) 69 *Past and Present* 50

Arden LJ, 'The Interpretation of UK Domestic Legislation in the Light of European Convention on Human Rights Jurisprudence' (2004) 25 *Statute Law Review* 170

Bennion, F., *Statutory Interpretation* (London: Butterworths, 3rd ed 1997)

Blackburn, R., *King and Country: Monarchy and the future King Charles III* (London: Politico's, 2005)

Bogdanor, V., *The Monarchy and the Constitution* (Oxford: Clarendon, 1995)

Bradford, S., *King George VI* (London: Weidenfeld and Nicolson, 1989)

Brazier, R., 'Legislating About the Monarchy' (2007) 66 *Cambridge Law Journal* 86

Campbell, Lady C., *The Royal Marriages: Private Lives of the Queen and her Children* (London: Smith Gryphon, 1993)

Cannadine, D., *The Pleasures of the Past* (London: Penguin, 1997)

Cranmer, F., 'Parliamentary report' (2009) 11 *Ecclesiastical Law Journal* 340

Cretney, S., 'The Royal Marriages Act 1772: A Footnote' (1995) 16 *Statute Law Review* 195

Cretney, S., 'The King and the King's Proctor: the abdication crisis and the divorce laws 1936-1937' (2000) 116 *Law Quarterly Review* 583

Cretney, S., *Family Law in the Twentieth Century: A History* (Oxford: Oxford University Press, 2003)

Cretney, S., 'The divorce law and the 1936 abdication crisis: a supplemental note' (2004) 120 *Law Quarterly Review* 163

Cretney, S., 'Royal Marriages: the Law in a Nutshell' [2005] *Family Law* 317

Cretney, S., 'Royal Marriages: Some Legal and Constitutional Issues' (2008) 124 *Law Quarterly Review* 218

Dillon, J., *Considerations on the Royal Marriages Act and on the Application of that Statute to a Marriage Contracted and Solemnized out of Great Britain* (London, 1811)

Dillon, J., *The Case of the Children of His Royal Highness the Duke of Sussex* (London, 1832)

Du Maurier, D., *Mary Anne* (London: Gollancz, 1954)

Eilers, M., *Queen Victoria's Descendants* (Falköping: Rosvall Royal Books, 1997)

Fabian Commission, *The Future of the Monarchy* (London: Fabian Society, 2003)

Farran, C. d'O., 'The Royal Marriages Act, 1772' (1951) 14 *Modern Law Review* 53

Fraser, F., *The Unruly Queen: The Life of Queen Caroline* (London: John Murray, 1996)

Fraser, F., *Princesses: The Six Daughters of George III* (London: John Murray, 2004)

Gardiner, J., *Queen Victoria* (London: Collins & Brown, 1997)

Gatrell, V., *City of Laughter: Sex and Satire in Eighteenth-Century London* (London: Atlantic Books, 2006)

Geary, N., *The Law of Marriage and Family Relations* (London and Edinburgh: Adam and Charles Black, 1892)

Gibson, E., *Codex juris ecclesiastici Anglicani* (London: 1713)

Gillis, J., *For Better, For Worse: British Marriages 1600 to the Present* (Oxford: Oxford University Press, 1985)

Glück Rosenthal, L., *A Biographical Memoir of his late Royal Highness the Duke of Sussex* (Brighton, 1846)

Gristwood, S., *Arbella: England's Lost Queen* (London: Bantam Press, 2003)

Harewood, Earl of, *The Tongs and the Bones: The Memoirs of Lord Harewood* (London: Weidenfeld & Nicolson, 1981)

Haw, R., *The State of Matrimony: An Investigation of the Relationship between Ecclesiastical and Civil Marriage after the*

Reformation, with a Consideration of the Laws relating thereto (London: SPCK, 1952)

Haydon, C., 'The Church in the Kineton deanery of the diocese of Worcester, c.1660-c.1800' in Gregory and Chamberlain (eds), *The National Church in Local Perspective: The Church of England and the Regions, 1660-1800* (Woodbridge: Boydell Press, 2003)

Hibbert, C., *George III: A Personal History* (London: Penguin, 1999)

Kavanagh, A., 'Statutory Interpretation and Human Rights After Anderson: A More Contextual Approach' (2004) *Public Law* 537

Lacey, R., *Majesty: Elizabeth II and the House of Windsor* (London: Hutchinson, 1977)

Lester, A., and Pannick, D., *Human Rights Law in Practice* (London: Butterworths, 2004)

Morris, B., 'The future of church establishment' (2010) 12 *Ecclesiastical Law Journal* 214

Mullen, R., 'The Last Wedding of a Prince of Wales, 1863' (1981) 31 *History Today* 10

Munson, J., *Maria Fitzherbert: The Secret Wife of George IV* (2001: London: Robinson, 2002)

Nissel, M., *People Count: A History of the General Register Office* (London: HMSO, 1987)

Parker, S., *Informal Marriage, Cohabitation and the Law, 1754-1989* (Basingstoke: Macmillan, 1990)

Parry, C., 'Further Considerations Upon the Prince of Hanover's Case' (1956) 5 *International and Comparative Law Quarterly* 61

Pickett, L., Prince, C., Prior, S., and Brydon, R., *War of the Windsors: A Century of Unconstitutional Monarchy* (London: Mainstream Publishing, 2002)

Pimlott, B., *The Queen: A Biography of Elizabeth II* (London: HarperCollins, 1996)

Pollock, F. and Maitland, F.W., *The History of English Law Before the Time of Edward I* (Cambridge: Cambridge University Press,

1923)

Probert, R., 'Lord Hardwicke's Marriage Act 250 years on: vital change?' [2004] *Family Law* 583

Probert, R., 'The wedding of the Prince of Wales: Royal Privileges and Human Rights' [2005] 17 *Child and Family Law Quarterly* 363

Probert, R., 'Common law marriage: myths and misunderstandings' [2008] 20 *Child and Family Law Quarterly* 1

Probert, R., *Marriage Law and Practice in the Long Eighteenth Century: A Reassessment* (Cambridge: Cambridge University Press, 2009)

Probert, R., 'Control over Marriage in England and Wales, 1753-1823: The Clandestine Marriages Act of 1753 in Context' (2009) 27 *Law and History Review* 413 (Probert 2009b)

Probert, R., 'Parental responsibility and children's partnership choices', in Probert, Herring and Gilmore (eds) *Responsible Parents and Parental Responsibility* (Oxford: Hart, 2009) (Probert 2009c)

Probert, R., 'The Roos case and modern family law' in Gilmore, Herring and Probert (eds), *Landmarks in Family Law* (Oxford: Hart, 2011)

Pugh, T.B., and Samuels, A., 'The Royal Marriages Act 1772; Its Defects and the Case for Repeal' (1994) 15 *Statute Law Review* 46

Schama, S., *A History of Britain Volume 3: The Fate of Empire, 1776-2000* (London: BBC Worldwide, 2002)

Shah-Kazemi, S., *Untying the Knot: Muslim Women, Divorce and the Shariah* (London: Nuffield Foundation, 2001)

Starkey, D., *Monarchy: From the Middle Ages to Modernity* (London: HarperCollins, 2006)

Tillyard, S., *A Royal Affair: George III and His Troublesome Siblings* (London: Vintage, 2006)

Tomalin, C., *Mrs Jordan's Profession: The story of a great actress and a future king* (London: Viking, 1994)

Townsend, P., *Time and Chance: An Autobiography* (London: Collins, 1978)

Trudgill, E., *Madonnas and Magdalens: The origin and development of Victorian sexual attitudes* (London; William Heinemann, 1976)

Waller, M., *Ungrateful Daughters: The Stuart Princesses Who Stole Their Father's Crown* (London: Sceptre, 2002)

Warwick, C., *Two Centuries of Royal Weddings* (London: Arthur Baker Ltd, 1980)

Weir, A., *Britain's Royal Families: The Complete Genealogy* (London: Pimlico, 1996)

Williams, J.A., 'English Catholicism under Charles II: The Legal Position' (1963) 7 *Recusant History* 123

Notes

(NA – 'National Archives,' Kew)

Chapter 1
1   Cannadine, p.2.
2   For a vivid account see Mullen.
3   See Pimlott, p.471.
4   Schama puts the figure at 'at least 800 million' (Schama, p.548)
5   Location of other royal weddings, including that of Prince Andrew and Sarah Ferguson on 23 July 1986.
6   See Probert 2005.
7   Laura Elston, Press Association, 16 November 2010.
8   This is the conclusion of Dr Stephen Cretney, who played a key role in drawing the issues to public notice in 2005: see Cretney 2008, p.249.
9   See e.g. Lacey, p.205, who describes the Royal Marriages Act as 'an embarrassment' but goes on to claim that 'it cannot actually prevent anyone doing what they really want to do' and to suggest that 'it only duplicates sanctions that exist in any case—to exclude unsuitable persons from the succession.' The Earl of Harewood, who had more reason than most to investigate the requirements of the law (see below, chs 3, 4), claimed in his autobiography that that the general law 'excludes anyone covered by the Royal Marriages Act' (Harewood, p.221.

A similar claim is made by Eilers, p.47. Just how inaccurate this is depends of course on the much-disputed scope of that Act—but it is clear that the overlap between the two pieces of legislation is not exact.
10 Dillon 1811, 2.
11 Dillon 1811, xiv.
12 While contemporary sources use the term 'divorce' to refer to annulments, and indeed separations, the conceptual distinction was clear.
13 See further Probert 2011.
14 See, for example, Glück Rosenthal, p.6.

Chapter 2
1   See generally Waller, ch.6.
2   Williams.
3   Haydon, p.167.
4   Starkey, p.160.
5   The Edict of Nantes was revoked in 1685, and thousands of Huguenot refugees fled to England.
6   See 'Royal Marriages—Constitutional Issues': House of Commons Library, SN/PC/03417.
7   Christopher Morgan, 'After 500 years, a royal wedding in the Vatican' *Sunday Times*, 5 November 2006.
8   Erin Baker, 'Sons follows Duchess of Kent into Catholicism' *Daily Telegraph*, 20 August 2001.
9   See, for example, the discussion of Marina Oglivy's mar-

riage to Paul Mowatt: 'Royals for a new Britain' *Sunday Times*, 4 February 1990.

10 Gardiner, p.60.

Chapter 3

1 Memorandum of 11 June 1956: NA CON 72/102.

2 Hibbert, p.352. In the light of such pronouncements, and his subsequent conduct, the claim that George had himself entered into a marriage with an obscure Quaker woman, Hannah Lightfoot, seems implausible, although see Weir, p.286.

3 Tillyard, p.292.

4 Hibbert, p.168.

5 Whether the marriage was actually valid is another issue: it was later alleged that Henry had gone through a ceremony of marriage with Olive Wilmot in 1767: see the claim by Olive's granddaughter Lavinia in NA HO 45/469 and see also Weir, p.281.

6 Munson, p.71.

7 Pugh and Samuels, p.48.

8 Tillyard, p.184.

9 Tillyard, p.182.

10 *The Grand Opinion for the Prerogative Concerning the Royal Family* (1717) Fortescue 401.

11 *Lords Journals*, 28 February 1772, col 270.

12 This was the case even in the sixteenth century when marrying without the monarch's consent was deemed to be high treason (on which see

The Grand Opinion, n.10 above). For an account of the incarceration of those who married without consent see e.g. Gristwood, describing how Arbella, a great-great-granddaughter of Henry VII, was sent to the Tower (where she later died) for secretly marrying William Seymour, and how Arbella's grandmother Margaret had herself been 'thrown into the Tower for an unsanctioned betrothal to Thomas Howard.'

13 Quoted by Tillyard, p.186.

14 Quoted by Dillon 1811, p.9.

15 Royal Marriages Act 1772, 12 Geo III c.11 s.1.

16 *Ibid*, section 2.

17 Probert 2009, ch.8.

18 *Sussex Peerage Case* (1844) 11 Cl & Fin 85, p.151.

19 Section 3.

20 Farran, p.55.

21 Fraser 2004, p.14.

22 Tillyard, p.85.

23 Tillyard, p.266.

24 Hibbert, p.352.

25 See generally Fraser 2004, pp.145, 280.

26 See Tomalin.

27 Du Maurier.

28 See generally Trudgill and Gatrell.

29 Munson, p.89.

30 *Ibid*, p.149. Some commentators have described the marriage to Mrs Fitzherbert as 'morganatic' (see e.g. Lacey, p.98), but this is not a concept recognized by English law. The

example of Mrs Fitzherbert was apparently constantly cited at the time of the abdication crisis (see e.g. Bradford, p.168), but it was hardly a promising one.

31 Although he would have been able to succeed to the throne of Hanover, which was not subject to the same religious restrictions.

32 Hibbert, p.370.

33 Pugh and Samuels, p.54.

34 Glück Rosenthal, pp.4, 49.

35 See e.g. *R v The Inhabitants of Brampton* (1808) 10 East 282.

36 The suit was instigated by Heseltine, the King's proctor, in the London Consistory Court: *Heseltine v Murray* (1794) 2 Addams 400n.

37 For a full exposition of the arguments, see e.g. Dillon 1811 and 1832.

38 Evidence produced in the *Sussex Peerage Case* (1844) 11 Cl & Fin 85, p.87.

39 Glück Rosenthal, p.5.

40 Dillon 1832, p.16, noting delicately that 'personal differences unfortunately arose between the parties.'

41 Fraser 2004, pp.189-191.

42 *Ibid*, pp.175, 183, 287.

43 *Ibid*, p.291.

44 Quoted by *ibid*, p.306.

45 Weir, p.288; Fraser 2004, p.263.

46 Fraser 2004, p.307.

47 Glück Rosenthal, p.12. Lady Cecilia was the ninth daughter of the Earl of Arran and the widow of Sir George Buggin. The marriage to Augustus took place in private, the assumption being that it took place at Great Cumberland Place on 2 May 1831 (Weir, p.295).

48 Fraser 2004, p.383.

49 Cretney 2008, p.225.

50 NA LO 2/975.

51 NA PC 8/250.

52 On the respective powers of the secular and church courts in this respect see e.g. *R v Inhabitants of Preston near Faversham* (1759) Burr. Sett. Cas. No. 154; *Robins v Crutchley* (1760) 2 Wils 118; *Ilderton v Ilderton* (1793) 2 H. Bl. 145.

53 See e.g. *Reid v Passer* (1794) 1 Esp. 213; *Leader v Barry* (1795) 1 Esp 353; *Evans v Morgan* (1832) 2 Cr & J 453; *Postman v Harrell* (1833) 6 C & P 225; *Woodgate v. Potts* (1847) 2 Car & Kir 457.

54 *Sussex Peerage Case* (1844) 11 Cl & Fin 85, p.145.

55 Thus, for example, when Prince Ernest of Cumberland was planning to marry Princess Victoria Louise of Prussia in 1913, it was agreed that the Foreign Office should communicate with his father 'calling attention to this effect of the Act in as delicate terms as possible, and intimating that HM would be ready to give the usual consent upon understanding that the Duke wishes it, in the same way as on the

occasion of the marriages of his two daughters' (NA PC 8/756). See also NA HO 45/8927 (marriage of Prince Royal of Hanover to Princess Mary of Saxe-Altenbourg).

56 Campbell, p.2; Warwick, p.25.

57 Otherwise known as Mary.

58 Eilers, p.44.

59 Starkey, p.302. For a rather un-flattering account, see Pickett *et al*, p.12.

60 Fabian Commission, p.94.

61 Eilers, p.45. The Titles Dep-rivation Act of 1917 further ensured that those with whom England was at war did not bear British royal titles.

62 Bradford, p.77.

63 Of course, they were already related to all of them by blood or marriage: Bradford, p.3.

64 See Gardiner, p.60.

65 Warwick, pp.23, 40.

66 Bradford, p.106.

67 Harewood, p.103.

68 Bradford, p.12. Mary had originally been betrothed to Prince Albert Victor, the eldest son of Edward VII, but he died in 1892 before the marriage could take place, and she subsequently married his younger brother, who succeeded to the throne as George V.

69 Weir, p.286.

70 NA LCO 2/8504.

71 Gardiner, p.57.

72 *Ibid*, p.55, quoting a letter in which she wrote that 'inde-pendent of my youth, and my great repugnance to change my present position, there is no anxiety evinced in this country for such an event, and it would be more prudent, in my opinion, to wait till some such demonstration is shown, - else if it were hurried it might produce discontent.'

73 Bradford, p.173. Correspond-ence in the National Archives makes it clear that it is the Cabinet, rather than the entire Privy Council, that needs to be consulted in such a case: see NA LCO 2/8504.

74 For a fascinating account see Cretney 2000.

75 See Bradford, p.185.

76 Lacey, p.74; Bradford, p.140.

77 Bradford, p.188; Bogdanor, p.248.

78 Bogdanor, pp.136-7.

79 His Majesty's Declaration of Abdication Act, section 1(3).

80 The marriage took place on 3 June 1937, one month after Wallis' divorce from Ernest Simpson had been made abso-lute: Cretney 2000, p.616.

81 Warwick, p.58.

82 NA CON 72/102. A further memorandum noted that '[w]hen the Queen became engaged in 1949 no formal advice was tendered by the Cabinet, who were told by the PM a few days before the an-nouncement' (HO 2901/87).

83 Townsend, p.206.

84 Cretney 2004.

85 Townsend had married

Rosemary Pawle in 1941, in what he later described as 'a typical wartime marriage,' and divorced in 1952: Townsend, pp.180, 194.

86 Pimlott, p.209.

87 Townsend, p.199.

88 NA LCO 2/5143.

89 NA LCO 2/6352 (memorandum of 3 March 1954).

90 Two years later consent was given (at a council held on the royal yacht) for Captain Ramsay to marry Miss Flora Fraser ('Royal Assent to Marriage' *Times*, 20 August 1956, p.8) and the marriage subsequently took place at St Peter's Episcopal Church, Fraserburgh (*Times*, 8 October 1956).

91 'Dr Fisher on Rumours About Princess An "Offensive Stunt"' *The Times*, 21 April 1955.

92 In the earlier case of *Heseltine v Murray* (1794) 2 Addams 400n, it is interesting to note how much weight was placed on the fact that Augustus was under the age of twenty-five at the time of his marriage to Lady Augusta Murray.

93 Royal Marriages Act, s.2.

94 Memo in NA LCO 2/6352.

95 *Ibid* (memo of 29 June 1955).

96 With the exception of any grandchildren 'by the marriage of a daughter to a foreigner' (NA LCO 2/6352).

97 There were differing views on this point: the Canadian High Commissioner suggested that this was not a matter on which other Commonwealth governments need be consulted (NA CON 72/102/1).

98 Townsend, p.224. It was an irony not lost upon those involved that Eden had himself divorced and remarried. His first marriage had ended on account of his wife's desertion, and he had married Clarissa in 1952. Four other members of his Cabinet had divorced, three of whom had subsequently remarried. One might imagine that this would have made them more sympathetic to Margaret's plight, but it might also have made them more cautious: the first—and to date only—divorced Prime Minister might well have wished to avoid any parallels being drawn.

99 NA PREM 11/1565.

100 See the discussion in Lacey, p.236.

101 Farran, p.59. For good measure, Farran pointed out that the descendants of George V would be 'doubly exempted', since his wife, Mary, was also a descendant of a British princess who had married into a foreign family.

102 Weir, p.284.

103 See for example the memo of June 1956 in NA LO 2/975. See also Parry, in which he expressed the view that it was 'impossible to accept that a person can be within both the rule and the exception.'

104 One argument against such an interpretation rests on a marriage that took place soon after the Act was passed. Had it been intended to exempt *all* the descendants in perpetuity of any princess who married into a foreign family, it is unlikely that its instigator King George III would have countenanced the marriage of his heir to Caroline of Brunswick. Caroline was the daughter of Princess Augusta, George III's eldest sister, who had married into a foreign family by marrying the Duke of Brunswick in 1764. It is hard to believe that George III, so unwilling to allow unsuitable matches, would have consented to a marriage which would have exempted the children of the very heir to the throne.

105 An Act for the Naturalization of the Most Excellent Princess Sophia, Electress & Duchess Dowager of Hanover, & the Issue of Her Body: 4 Anne c.4.

106 The Act naturalizing the descendants of Princess Sophia was of course passed before the Act of Union with Scotland in 1707, but this distinction was not a point pressed by the Attorney-General. He noted that while the Act of Union did not specifically provide that all subjects of England and of Scotland were to become subjects of the United Kingdom, this was to be assumed: *Attorney-General v Prince Ernest Augustus of Hanover* [1957] A.C. 436.

107 *A-G v Prince Ernest* [1957] A.C. 436, p.461.

108 Letter of 17 November 1955 (NA LO 2/975).

109 On the interrelatedness of the royal families of Europe see e.g. the 'Royal Oak' depicting the family tree of Victoria and Albert and their contribution to the royal houses of Europe: Gardiner, p.137.

110 Princess Alice married Louis IV Grand Duke of Hesse, and her daughter married the first Marquess of Milford Haven. It was thought unnecessary to give consent to the latter marriage, or those of subsequent descendants.

111 Of course, these hypothetical doubts over Prince Philip's legitimacy were further complicated by the legal effect of illegitimacy in previous generations: the first marriage celebrated without the necessary consent would be void, and so the next generation would be illegitimate under the Royal Marriages Act, but this in turn would presumably take that generation out of the scope of the Act, and subsequent marriages could not therefore be invalidated for lack of consent (though questions over royal status might in turn be raised). The

point was made by a Mr Dermot Morrah in a letter to *The Times* on 18 November 1955.

112 NA LO 2/975.

113 The provisions of the Act only applied to those born after 28 October 1959.

114 For a full account of the passage of the 1959 Act see Cretney 1995.

115 NA PREM 11/3093 (labelled 'top secret' and described as 'very difficult territory'). The file is full of notices stating that minutes have been extracted and will not be available to the public, and the initial closure period of 50 years has been extended to 100.

116 'Harewood Divorce Suit: Woman Named in Petition' *The Times*, 3 January 1967, p.1.

117 Lacey, p.319.

118 In July 1964: Harewood, p.219.

119 Lacey, p.319.

120 *Hansard* (HC) 5th Series vol 741, col 1426.

121 Pimlott, p.374.

122 Bogdanor, p.56; Harewood, p.221.

123 Harewood, p.102.

124 Eilers, p.45.

125 Blackburn, p.42.

126 Pugh and Samuels, p.58.

127 Christopher Morgan, above note 7 to ch.2.

128 *Sussex Peerage Case* (1844) 11 Cl & Fin 85, p.93.

129 The relevant section was repealed by the Criminal Law Act 1967, Sch 4. See further

the memo of 29 December 1965 that this was 'merely a matter of statute law revision' and did not affect the succession.

Chapter 4

1 Clandestine Marriages Act 1753, s.17.

2 On the terminology of 'common law' in this context, see Probert 2008.

3 For a full discussion, see Probert 2009.

4 Canon 103 of the Canons of 1603: Gibson, p.515.

5 A point raised by the judges in 1717: *The Grand Opinion for the Prerogative Concerning the Royal Family* (1717) Fortescue 401.

6 Hibbert, p.167.

7 Tillyard, p.303.

8 C.f. Munson, p.82, who suggested that the 1753 Act would have invalidated the marriage.

9 Canon 62.

10 *Wynn v Davies* (1835) 1 Curt 69; 163 ER 24.

11 Geary, p.117.

12 Weir, p.278.

13 Fraser 1996, p.61.

14 Warwick, p.11.

15 *Ibid*, p.12.

16 Marriage Act 1822, 3 Geo IV c.75, s.23; Marriage Act 1823, 4 Geo IV c.76, s.30.

17 Section 18.

18 Section 20.

19 Probert 2009, ch.5.

20 Sections 4 and 6.

21 Section 14.

22 Marriage Act 1836, s.45.

23 See Anderson.

24 Section 6.

25 Nissel, p.15.

26 See Tomalin; Fraser 1996.

27 (1843-44) 10 Cl & F 534; 11 ER 844.

28 The marriage laws in force in Ireland at a time of bitter religious division formed a bewilderingly complex web. Although there was legislation governing the marriages of Catholics by Catholic priests, or of Presbyterians by Presbyterian ministers, or of any couples married by a member of the Established Church, there was no statutory provision for a valid marriage between a member of the Established Church and a Presbyterian if the marriage was celebrated by a Presbyterian minister. As a result, the matter had to be determined by reference to the pre-statute canon law.

29 See also Pollock and Maitland, p.372.

30 For the assertion that members of the royal family may contract a 'common-law' marriage see e.g. Blackburn, p.59.

31 Warwick, p.22.

32 Westminster Abbey, not being a parish church, was at the time only occasionally used for weddings. There had been on average scarcely more than one each year since the turn of the century, generally of people connected in some way with the life of the Abbey. One month before Princess Patricia's marriage in 1919, for example, the daughter of a viscount had married a clerk in Holy Orders.

33 Or rather, as one royal biographer has pointed out, of Schleswig-Holstein-Sonderburg-Glücksburg: Bradford, p.141.

34 Weir, pp.324-5; Lacey, p.33.

35 'Forthcoming Marriages', *The Times*, 18 January 1941.

36 NA HO 144/21548.

37 Memo of 21 February 1941: NA LO3/1235.

38 *Ibid.*

39 Memorandum of 17 February 1941: NA HO 144/21548.

40 Letter of 3 March 1941: NA HO 144/21548. Sir Rupert was the clerk to the Privy Council and as such the most senior civil servant in the Privy Council Office.

41 The Act provided that '[i]f at any time it appears to the Lord Chancellor to be expedient that a Bill should be prepared for the purpose of consolidating the enactments relating to any subject, but that, in order to facilitate the consolidation of those enactments, he may cause to be laid before Parliament a memorandum proposing such corrections and minor improvements therein as he thinks to be expedient' (s. 1(1)). Provision was made for these amendments to be

publicized (s. 1(2)). The draft Bill, together with the Lord Chancellor's memorandum and any representations made, were then referred to a joint committee of both Houses of Parliament. All corrections and minor improvements had to be approved by the Committee with the concurrence of the Lord Chancellor and the Speaker of the House of Commons (s. 1(3) and (4)).

42 Sixth Report of the Joint Select Committee on Consolidation Bills, 1948-9 BPP vol 6 (London: HMSO, 1949), pp.1-2.

43 Consolidation of Enactments (Procedure) Act, s.2.

44 Section 1(5).

45 Section 79(5).

46 For details of the minor amendments see the discussion in Cretney 2003, pp.23-4.

47 See Bennion, p.465, and note the comments of Lord Upjohn in *Beswick v Beswick* [1968] AC 58.

48 See e.g. NA HO 144/19713, discussing the arrangements for the marriage of the Duke of Kent to Princess Marina of Greece.

49 NA HO 45/24303.

50 Section 2.

51 Section 3.

52 Section 1 and Schedule 1.

53 Memorandum of 15 December 1948: NA HO 45/24303.

54 Memorandum of 29 June 1955: NA LCO 2/6352.

55 Draft Memorandum to the Cabinet by the Lord Chancellor, 29 October 1955.

56 Statement issued on 31 October 1955.

57 Harewood, p.221.

58 *Ibid.*

59 *Ibid*, p.222.

60 *Ibid*, p.223.

61 *The Times* 28 February 1998.

62 Eilers, p.137.

63 When Marina Oglivy married Paul Mowatt in 1990, it was initially reported that the ceremony was to take place in a register office; it in fact took place at Ham Common Church ('Royals for a new Britain' *Sunday Times*, 4 February 1990).

64 Warwick, p.138.

65 M. Nash, 'Floundering in the mud of history' *Sunday Times* 13 December 1992. See also Campbell, p.237 ('the Royal Family are forbidden to marry in an English Register Office').

Chapter 5

1 *Rees v UK* (1987) 9 EHRR 56, at para 50.

2 *Hamer v UK* (1979) 24 DR 5, para 62; *Draper v UK* (1980) 24 DR 72, para 49.

3 *Donoghue v UK*, App. no 34848/07, decided 14 December 2010.

4 Human Rights Act 1998, s.6.

5 Human Rights Act 1998, s.4.

6 *Bellinger v Bellinger* [2003] UKHL 21.

7 Lord Bingham of Cornhill, in *R (on the application of Baiai*

and others) v Secretary of State for the Home Department [2008] UKHL 53 para 30. That this would indeed breach the Convention was confirmed by the ECHR in *Donoghue v UK*.

8 *Diego Andres Aguilar Quila, Amber Aguilar, Shakira Bibi, Suhyal Mohammed v Secretary of State for the Home Department* [2010] EWCA Civ 1482.

9 *Quila*, at para 31.

10 Gender Recognition Act 2004.

11 The House of Lords delivered their judgment in *Bellinger v Bellinger* on 10 April 2003 and the Gender Recognition Act 2004 came into force on 4 April 2005. In the meantime, a male-to-female transsexual could marry a woman, but not a man.

12 Proceedings were brought by the AIRE Centre and the Joint Council for the Welfare of Immigrants: see *Donoghue v UK*, above note 3.

13 See e.g. *The Guardian* 10 December 1992.

14 'Ministers were told that civil marriage would not be legal' *The Times*, 9 June 2006, p.2.

15 E. Hardcastle, *Daily Mail* 21 August 2001.

16 For an account of the work behind the scenes, see the statement issued by Stephen Cretney on 20 February 2005, commending the 'care and thoroughness' with which the matter had been researched and the 'concern for scrupu-

lous accuracy' displayed by those involved.

17 Stephen Bates, 'Blunders cast a shadow over big day for Charles and Camilla' *The Guardian*, 23 February 2005.

18 Marriage (Approved Premises) Regulations 1995, Sch 2 para 7 and Sch 1 para 2 respectively.

19 Cretney 2005. The matter was therefore not quite such a 'trivial' one as the Prince's champion, Jonathan Dimbleby, later claimed ('Utterly at ease and brimming with affection' *The Times*, 8 April 2005).

20 Caroline Davies, 'Charles cannot marry at Windsor Castle' *Daily Telegraph*, 18 February 2005.

21 'So whose head will roll?' *Daily Telegraph*, 27 February 2005.

22 This is the explanation proffered by Jonathan Dimbleby, see above note 19.

23 Simon Walters, 'Charles Wedding Illegal Warn Experts', *Mail on Sunday*, 20 February 2005.

24 Joshua Rozenberg, 'Civil marriage will be legal, say prince's aides' *Daily Telegraph*, 15 February 2005.

25 P. Naughton, 'Lord Chancellor rules that royal wedding is legal' *The Times*, 23 February 2005.

26 'Charlie Falconer presents Times Law awards' *The Times*, 1 March 2005, p.7.

27 Stephen Cretney's *Family Law in the Twentieth Century: A History*, drawing on extensive research in the National Archives, had been published in 2003. Two articles on the abdication crisis had been published in the *Law Quarterly Review*, and an earlier piece on the Royal Marriages Act had been published in the *Statute Law Review*.

28 Written Ministerial Statement, *Hansard* (HL) 24 February 2005 col WS87.

29 Given that those advising on a possible marriage between Margaret and Townsend in 1955 were adamant that members of the royal family could not marry in a civil marriage in England and Wales, it is clear that the 1953 Act was not thought to make any difference to the availability of such a ceremony.

30 While, as we have seen, scholars had long been critical of the (perfectly correct) decision of the House of Lords that the presence of an Anglican minister was necessary for a marriage even prior to 1754, it was the work of John Gillis and Stephen Parker in the 1980s that popularized the idea that 'informal' marriages were common before 1754 (see Gillis; Parker).

31 See Probert 2009, ch.3, 7; see also Probert 2005.

32 Joshua Rozenberg, 'Camilla may have no choice but to be Queen' *Daily Telegraph*, 17 February 2005.

33 Bennion, pp.558-9.

34 'Falconer: the marriage is lawful' *The Guardian*, 24 February 2005, although contrast Ben Sheppard, 'Do these 1955 papers show wedding IS illegal?' *Mail on Sunday*, 27 February 2005, p.8.

35 'Charlie, the perfect man to finish Charles' *The Times*, 27 February 2005.

36 Caroline Davies, 'Prince's wedding saved by Human Rights Act' *Daily Telegraph*; Sandra Laville and Clare Dyer, 'Human Rights to the rescue of wedding' *The Guardian*; Tom Baldwin and Frances Gibb, 'Charles relies on rights law he despised to validate marriage' *The Times* (all 24 February 2005).

37 Laville and Dyer, above.

38 'Royal blunders descend to farce' *Daily Mail*, 24 February 2005.

39 'So is Lord Falconer right?' *Daily Mail*, 24 February 2005.

40 Baldwin and Gibb, above n.36.

41 Sam Coates, Philip Webster and Frances Gibb, 'Tories back Bill to dispel legal doubts over royal wedding' *The Times*, 25 February 2005.

42 Simon Walters, 'I thought British people were supposed to be compassionate. I don't see it' *Mail on Sunday*, 27 February 2005, p.8.

43 'So whose head will roll?' above note 21.

44 James Meek, 'Turbulent priest' *The Guardian*, 25 February 2005.

45 Kunal Dutta, 'Letters and caveats: How to object' *The Guardian*, 25 February 2005.

46 Andrew Pierce, 'Vicar wins royal wedding inquiry' *The Times*, 2 March 2005.

47 Statement from Len Cook, Registrar General for England and Wales, issued 8 March.

48 The reference to the Marriage Act 1994 added nothing to the overall argument: this inserted new provisions into the 1949 Act to enable civil ceremonies to take place in a wider range of venues than previously. Under these provisions Windsor Castle could have been approved for the celebration of civil marriages, but the finer detail—and the consequences of such approval—had clearly been overlooked at the time of the announcement.

49 'Letters' [2005] *Family Law* 507.

50 Stephen Bates and Martin Wainwright, 'Royal wedding gets legal stamp of approval' *The Guardian*; Sally Pook, 'Royal marriage can go ahead, says registrar' *Daily Telegraph*, both 9 March 2005.

51 Jane Simpson, 'Secret of Charles' Scottish Wedding' *Mail on Sunday*, 20 March 2005.

52 See e.g. James Chapman, 'Margaret papers cast a shadow on Charles' wedding' *Daily Mail*, 30 March 2005.

53 Isabelle Chevallot, 'Hurdles on the way to the wedding day' *The Guardian*, 5 April 2005; Caroline Davies, 'Just the latest in a series of setbacks in build-up to the big day' *Daily Telegraph*, 5 April 2005.

54 'Ministers were told that civil marriage would not be legal' *The Times*, 9 June 2006.

55 Ref. FS50225088.

56 See paras 22 and 24 of the Ministerial Code, July 2001, and paras 2.10 and 2.13 of the current Code, July 2007.

57 12 April 2010.

58 Sarah Wescott, 'Prince Charles and Camilla: "Cover-Up" Over Legality of Marriage' *Daily Express*, 12 April 2010.

59 Walesonline.co.uk.

60 Michael Thornton, 'For once, Charles, do your duty. Let William be our next King?' *Daily Mail*, 19 November 2010.

61 See e.g. Gordon Rayner, 'Queen Camilla; A "slip of the tongue" by the Prince of Wales has raised the question of his wife's title when he becomes king' *Daily Telegraph*, 23 November 2010.

62 'Camilla "could" be the Queen admits Charles' *Daily Express*, 20 November 2010.

63 See e.g. *Piers v Piers* (1849) 2 HL Cas 331; *Sichel v Lambert* (1864) 15 C.B. (N.S.) 781;

Mahadervan v Mahadervan [1964] P 233. Of course, the very nature of a legal presumption is that it is rebuttable, and *Collett v Collett* [1968] P 482 emphasises that the ceremony itself must be one that is sufficient to constitute a valid marriage.

64 It would, of course, be unduly cynical to suggest that any reliance was placed upon this by those advising the Prince.

65 Written Ministerial Statement.

66 *Rees v UK* (1987) 9 EHRR 56, at para 50.

67 See A. Thorpe, *The Human Rights Bill (HL), Bill 119 of 1997-98: Churches and Religious organisations* (House of Commons Library, 1998), Research Paper 98/26.

68 *Hansard* (HC) vol 312 col 1017, 20 May 1998.

69 'Advice to the Clergy', Annex 1 of GS 1449.

70 'Charles gets his vicar's blessing to remarry' *Daily Telegraph*, 4 April 2003.

71 Marriage (Scotland) Act 1977, s.18, as amended by the Marriage (Scotland) Act 2002, s.1. For further details see Marriage (Approval of Places) (Scotland) Regulations 2002, SSI No 260/2002

72 See Arden.

73 *Baiai*, above note 7.

74 Lester and Pannick, para 4.12.6.

75 See Bogdanor, p.44.

76 Section 79(5).

77 Simon Walters, above note 23.

78 The same point applies to suggestions that Parliament could have passed legislation allowing the marriage to take place at Windsor Castle without the need for it to be designated as 'approved premises' (see e.g. Marcel Berlins, 'How Charles and Camilla missed a trick, and a legally binding gift of semen' *The Guardian*, 8 March 2005). The argument was ingenious but missed the crucial point that it would be difficult to justify special treatment for royalty at the same time as arguing for equality.

79 'Let's hear it for mad monarchy' *The Observer*, 25 January 2009.

80 Kavanagh, p.545.

81 Earlier commentators had raised the point that the 1772 Act 'may conflict with the European Convention': Pugh and Samuels, p.58.

82 Nicholas Hellen and Christopher Morgan, 'Church objects to TV royal wedding' *The Times*, 27 February 2005.

83 Recent royal weddings celebrated according to Anglican rites include that of Lady Rose Windsor, the younger daughter of the Duke of Gloucester, who in 2008 was married in the Queen's Chapel, St James's, by the Reverend William Scott. Amelia May Beaumont, a great-great-great-great-granddaughter of

Queen Victoria, was married in the Temple Church in 2007 by Reverend Robin Griffith-Jones, and Lord Frederick Windsor, son of Prince Michael of Kent, was married by the Right Reverend Richard Chartres, Bishop of London, in the Chapel Royal at Hampton Court in 2009.

84 Marriage and Registration Acts Amendment Act 1856: see Haw.

85 Christopher Morgan, above note 7, ch.2.

86 Alison Bellamy, 'Royal wedding staged at Harewood House' *Yorkshire Evening Post*, 21 April 2009.

87 He and his elder sister Emily, were also outside the application of the Royal Marriages Act, and so did not require the Queen's consent to marry, although both asked for and were given consent to their marriages.

88 Cretney 2008, p.221.

Chapter 6

1 Marriage Act 1994, inserting new provisions into the Marriage Act 1949.

2 *Baiai*, above note 7, ch.5.

3 *Quila*, above note 8, ch.5.

4 See further Probert 2009, ch.8.

5 See further Probert, 2009b.

6 Save where a marriage is knowingly and willfully celebrated after a parent or guardian has objected to its going ahead: see further Prob-

ert 2009c.

7 Anderson, p.64.

8 See Bogdanor.

9 'PM and Palace "discussed reform"' BBC News, 27 March 2009.

10 Cranmer, p.343.

11 See Andrew Brown, 'Catholics hail Duchess of Kent's conversion' *The Independent*, 12 January 1994. See also Eilers, p.46 on the conversion to Catholicism of the Duchess of Gloucester.

12 A point made by Edward Leigh MP, Conservative MP for Gainsborough, when seeking leave to bring the Royal Marriages (Freedom of Religion) Bill into the House of Commons: see *Hansard* (HC) 8 March 2005, vol 431 col 1393.

13 *Sussex Peerage Case* (1844) 11 Cl & Fin 85.

14 See pp.70-72

15 Pugh and Samuels, p.58, and Farran for alternative interpretations of this exemption

16 NA PREM 11/1565.

17 Eilers, p.158; Weir, p.311.

18 Eilers, p.45.

19 For details see Eilers, pp.124, 129, 131-2, 134, 143-4, 146-8, 151, 158, 168.

20 As Pugh and Samuels at p.58 point out, the Act certainly applies to at least some foreign nationals.

21 'Difference of Opinion' *The Guardian* 24 February 2005.

22 *Hansard* (HL) 23 March 2005, col 237

23 Morris, p.215.

24 Letter of 25 October 1948: NA HO 45/24303.

25 Memo of 18 June 1952 by Sir Alan Lascelles: NA LCO 2/6352.

26 Letter of 8 June 1953: NA LCO 2/6352. The coronation had taken place only six days earlier, and the by-play between Princess Margaret and Peter Townsend had sparked speculation about their relationship.

27 Letter of 20 December 1955: NA CON 72/102.

28 Brazier, p.87.

29 The Succession to the Crown Bill was introduced in the Lords on 8 December 2004, and was debated on 14 January 2005, while the Succession to the Crown Bill (No 2) was introduced in the Commons on 12 January 2005. A third and slightly different bill, the Royal Marriages (Freedom of Religion) Bill, was introduced in the Commons on 8 March 2005 by Edward Leigh MP.

30 *Hansard* (HC Deb) 27 March 2009, col 621 et seq.

31 The date set for the resumption of the debate on the second reading was 16 October 2009, almost seven months later. In the event the debate was not resumed due to objections from MPs (a common fate for private members' bills: see *Hansard* (HC Deb) 16 October 2009, vol 497 col 608).

32 See, for example, Lord Falconer's statement that the government had no plans to legislate, on the basis that legislation 'is not needed at the moment as there is no practical discriminatory effect on the current line of royal succession' (*Hansard* (HL) 14 January 2005, vol 668, col 512).

33 See, for example, the comments of the then Justice Secretary, Jack Straw, in response to a query about the government's plans to amend the Act of Succession: 'To bring about changes to the law on succession would be a complex undertaking involving amendment or repeal of a number of items of related legislation, as well as requiring the consent of legislatures of member nations of the Commonwealth. We are examining this complex area although there are no immediate plans to legislate' (*Hansard* (HC) 12 January 2009, vol 486, col 513W).

34 See, for example, the discussion of the Royal Marriages (Freedom of Religion) Bill: *Hansard* (HC) 8 March 2005, vol 431, col 1393.

35 *Hansard* (HL) 14 January 2005, vol 668, col 514.

36 Cretney 2008, pp.220, 221.

37 Lacey, p.109.

38 *Hansard* (HC) 12 January 2009, vol 486, col 513W.

39 See further Probert 2004.

40 ONS, *Civil Registration: Vital*

Change - Birth, Marriage and Death Registration in the Twenty-First Century (2002) Cm 5355.

41 The White Paper *Civil Registration: Delivering Vital Change*, published by the ONS in 2003, indicated that reform was to be carried out under the Regulatory Reform Act 2001. The draft Regulatory Reform Order presented to Parliament on 22 July 2004 dealt only with the registration of births and deaths, but even this more limited reform was thought by the relevant Parliamentary committees to be an inappropriate use of the 2001 Act (House of Lords Select Committee on Delegated Powers and Regulatory Reform, *Third Report: Proposal for the draft Regulatory Reform (Registration of Births and Deaths) (England and Wales) Order 2004*; House of Commons Select Committee on Regulatory Reform, *Second Report*, paras 50 and 55). Following this rejection it was announced that the procedure would not be used for the planned reforms to marriage law either (Ministerial Statement on the Modernisation of Civil Registration, 1 March 2005).

42 ONS, *Marriage, Divorce and Adoption Statistics 2007* (2010).

43 Annex to the Law Commission's *Report on Solemnization of Marriage in England and Wales* (1973) (Law Com No 53), para 4.

44 See e.g. the varying outcomes of *Gereis v Yagoub* [1997] 1 FLR 854 (marriage held to be void); *Chief Adjudication Officer v Bath* [2000] 1 FLR 8 (marriage presumed to be valid); *A-M v A-M* [2001] 2 FLR 6 (couple presumed to have married overseas); *Gandhi v Patel* [2001] 1 FLR 603 (non-marriage).

45 See e.g. Shah-Kazemi on Muslim marriages.

46 Bogdanor, p.60.

47 NA LCO 2/6352.

Lightning Source UK Ltd.
Milton Keynes UK
14 March 2011

169236UK00001B/28/P